64⁹

An out of the ordinary parenting book which combines practical know-how with deep psychological knowledge. Writing with a deceptive lightness of touch, Caroline Penney helps us to understand the reasons why both parents and children behave as they do. A very welcome book.

Dr Sue Gerhardt, author of *Why Love Matters*

Surviving family life is a big challenge, yet good-enough parenting can go a long way to refuting poet Philip Larkin's infamous claim that mum and dad 'f*** up' their children. This splendid new book will greatly assist parents in negotiating the parenting minefield successfully, helping them to raise emotionally balanced, happy children.

Oliver James, psychologist, psychotherapist and writer

The Parenting Toolkit is a comprehensive guide to parenting from a developmental perspective. Penney uses her many years of experience working with children and families to address the multifaceted tasks that face parents of children and adolescents. The author appreciates that the central fact about children is that they are growing, physically, mentally, emotionally and socially. Her discussions of healthy practices for children and youth are buttressed by research and many anecdotes from her own clinical practice. Parents will find this a handy, and helpful, guide to read as a whole, or to return to when dealing with any of the parenting issues discussed in the book. It is an essential manual for parents of children at all age levels.

David Elkind, Ph.D. Professor Emeritus of Child Development, Tufts University

A small book, large in ideas, themes, and strategies to facilitate both the parent–child relationship and also the child's integrated development. A tool-kit well stocked with examples, exercises, and stories, likely to be of great value for parents in mobilizing their creativity, confidence, reflective functioning, and continuing engagement with their child over the peaks and valleys of family life.

Dr Dan Hughes, Psychologist and Founder of Dyadic Developmental Psychotherapy (DDP)

An interesting and informative book, filled with practical life examples, giving easy pictures of how to engage with our children without stress. There are many exercises for managing behaviour, listening to our children, stress management (of our and our children's lives) and general parenting hints and tips. The examples of how we adults can work on our own behaviours and responses in order to support our children are very practical. There are also ideas for working with our friends, setting up family support groups, and listening to children, amongst others. An appendix contains some very interesting information on the theories that underpin parenting. Throughout, beautiful illustrations embellish the chapters and examples, making a delightful addition to the book.

Janni Nicol, Early Childhood Executive Officer, Steiner Waldorf Schools Fellowship, UK

Hardware and DIY shops are among my favorite places to hang out. While I might not understand what to do with some of the items, I am grateful for the multiplicity of tools available for the variety of things needing to be repaired or re-built. This mirrors the relief that will be experienced by parents and educators when they read Caroline Penney's The Parenting Toolkit. There is no one-size-fits-all approach to raising happy children, to self-care, to discipline, parenting styles, or stress management.

Brilliantly, Penney offers a variety of strategies to bring to each of these topics and more. One does not need to agree with every strategy as there are others from which to choose that can bring about healthy and joyful results. She also reminds us that we need to take into account the ages and stages of development of the children. What works for a ten-year-old is not the approach to take with a young child or a teenager. Her many years as a family therapist and parenting expert, as well as her own experiences as a parent and grandparent, offer depth and authenticity to this practical and warm-hearted manual. Add this to your parent library now.

Cynthia Aldinger, author of *Life Is the Curriculum* and *Home Away From Home*

Modernity has heralded the loss of much intuitive wisdom about good-enough parenting – further exacerbated by a general crisis of stability and continuity in the modern family. Caroline Penney's expert distillation of decades of clinical experience will greatly empower parents; and as a template for helping children to thrive, this book could hardly be bettered.

Richard House Ph.D. chartered psychologist, childhood campaigner, editor of *Too Much, Too Soon?*

The Parenting Toolkit is practical and easy to use, and packed full of useful ideas for new and experienced parents. The Toolkit sparkles with the author's joyful experience of children, parents and family life and her understanding of the demands and difficulties involved. I thoroughly recommend it.

Dr Crispin Day, Psychologist and Head of Centre for Parent and Child Support, South London and Maudsley NHS Foundation Trust

Caroline Penney's years of experience with parents shine through this wonderful book. Inspired by her early experience of Parent Network, she has built on this with tried and tested ideas from family therapy, all brought to life with vivid examples and stories.

Doro Marden, former Parent Network Chair and author of *Raise Happy Children: Teach Yourself*

The Parenting Toolkit

simple steps to happy & confident children

Hawthorn Press

The Parenting Toolkit © 2018 Caroline Penney.

Caroline Penney is hereby identified as the author of this work in accordance with section 77 of the Copyright, Designs and Patent Act, 1988. She asserts and gives notice of her moral right under this Act.

Hawthorn Press

Published by Hawthorn Press, Hawthorn House,
1 Lansdown Lane, Stroud, Gloucestershire, GL5 1BJ, UK
Tel: (01453) 757040   Email: info@hawthornpress.com
www.hawthornpress.com

Design by Lucy Guenot
Illustrations by Kate Hajducka
Printed by Short Run Press Ltd, Exeter

Every effort has been made to trace the ownership of all copyrighted material. If any omission has been made, please bring this to the publisher's attention so that proper acknowledgement may be given in future editions.

The views expressed in this book are not necessarily those of the publisher.

Printed on environmentally friendly chlorine-free paper sourced from renewable forest stock.

British Library Cataloguing in Publication Data applied for.

ISBN 978-1-907359-90-3

The Parenting Toolkit

simple steps to happy & confident children

Caroline Penney

Hawthorn Press

Contents

Dedication

In loving memory of my parents Tony and Annette Freud who would have shared my pleasure in the publication of this book.

To Robert, Jessica and Nicholas who are my best teachers in how to be a parent and for all the love and joy you bring to my life.

To Lawrence for your wisdom and support.

Foreword

The very best parent I know had a terrible childhood. Her family was violent, desperately poor, and chaotic. Too many children, too little time and space. Kids fixed their own meals half the time, and they often woke to find strangers asleep in their living room or wandering down the hallway. It wasn't that her parents didn't care; they were just totally out of their depth. It was like being children raised by children.

Somehow, I don't know how, she managed to figure out all the things wrong with her childhood, and made sure that her own children had the opposite – stability, affection, fun, and discipline that was friendly and never scary.

You don't have to have a good childhood to be able to parent well. But you do need the chance to reflect, think and get in touch with what it felt like to be a child, and what might make things better.

There are an awful lot of books on raising kids, and a million self-proclaimed experts on the internet, with cheery lists of tips and points to make your child resilient, successful, confident, and so on. I am sure this is worthy stuff, but it makes me want to get my kayak out and sail right away. A snowstorm of advice is not what parents need.

Caroline's book is deeper water than this. It uses the secrets that family therapists know to get underneath problems and unlock what is causing them. Are you neglecting self-care? Are there emotional areas that press your buttons and make it hard to stay calm? Was your childhood a nightmare that seems to come back and haunt you and mess up your life even now?

In clear, simple and friendly language, she helps you understand and overcome these hurdles. She tells you the kind of stories I love to hear – the ones about families in much worse trouble than you, or at least as bad, and how they untangled things and went on to have happier lives.

There are ways to think about what you do and say to kids which are better than what was done and said to us when we were growing up. It's not mysterious or hard. If you can change the wheel on a car, or find your way around Netflix, or make pancakes on a Saturday morning, you can learn to communicate with kids.

I would recommend taking this book in small bits. Try some of it out, and see if it makes a difference. You've got all the time in the world, as your kids will keep giving you new chances to improve!

Most people are good at some parts of being a mum or dad, but have holes in their abilities. Some aspects of parenthood just seem to go wrong, or blow up in our faces. You will naturally notice chapter titles that grab your attention, because you know, at some level, what you need to be more able to relax and be more connected with yourself and your kids. The whole human race is on this journey of healing and learning.

It took generations to get this messed up, and if we can shine even a bit of light into ourselves and grow a bit warmer and clearer, we can be very proud. Enjoy this book. Enjoy parenthood. That's why we do it, and why it can feel so good when we get it right.

Steve Biddulph
Tasmania, 2018

Introduction

Many parents tell me that they wish that they'd been given an instruction manual when they had a baby. Many of us felt completely unprepared at first for parenthood, feeling that we had to 'make it up as we went along'. *The Parenting Toolkit* is that manual we all wish we'd had.

Raising a child is one the most important and complicated activities anyone will ever do. This book gives you 12 basic parenting principles to help get it right. These principles help to improve the relationship between you and your child, provide strategies for dealing with challenging times and behaviour, and help your parenting to become more satisfying, fun and rewarding. They will help all your family to get along better, and increase the confidence and self-esteem of your children.

The Parenting Toolkit is based on how I have helped hundreds of families in my professional and clinical practice as a family therapist, on the latest research in the area, and – very importantly – on my own experience as the mother of three children. It is about becoming a reflective parent instead of just reacting to situations as they happen. It is about making the often small changes in how you relate to your child that can result in dramatic transformations in your family life.

How to use this book

I would recommend that you first read the book straight through, which will give you a full understanding of the whole Parenting Toolkit. Then you could spend more time going over each chapter and doing the associated exercises. Each chapter builds on the understanding from the previous one.

However, if you are short of time, you may wish just to look at one aspect of parenting that interests you, such as child-led play or the meaning of children's behaviour – in which case you can jump to those chapters. As your children grow and develop, the chapter on ages and stages will be fascinating, and the chapter on discipline strategies would be useful if you feel you need to update your knowledge on effective discipline methods.

If you work with parents you may like to investigate the appendix on the theories that underpin parenting education.

The book can also be used as a reference book, to dip into and out of when you are uncertain how to handle a specific issue, and the examples illustrating problems can show how making small adjustments to your parenting can achieve transformational results.

With a pencil in hand it could also be used as a work book in which you can learn about your child, and perhaps about yourself.

The book covers the following topics:

1. **Looking after yourself.** This chapter looks at the importance of getting your own needs met as a parent and not to feel guilty about this. It also looks at how patterns from previous generations can influence how we parent, arguing that these need to be understood so that we do not pass on unhelpful patterns of parenting.

2. **Feelings.** This chapter describes the importance of acknowledging feelings so children feel that their feelings are being taken seriously. It also helps parents understand how to express feelings in a way that can be heard and does not spoil relationships.

3. **Child-led play.** This chapter explains the reasons why play is important and how to implement child-led play so the child experiences high-quality special time with their parent(s).

4. **Parenting styles.** This chapter describes the main types of parenting style – Aggressive, Passive, Manipulative and Assertive – and their impact on children.

5. **Descriptive praise.** This chapter describes how to give specific praise which helps the child feel valued.

6. **Labels.** This chapter looks at the importance of not ascribing labels to children, but describing the behaviour instead. It also looks at roles in the family and the importance of letting children not be defined by a role – e.g. the 'sporty' one or the 'shy' one.

7. **Helping your child solve problems.** This chapter describes how a parent can help their child solve problems in a creative way.

8. **Understanding your child's behaviour.** This chapter explains that no behaviour occurs in a vacuum. There is always a need underlying the behaviour, and this behaviour is always communicating a meaning.

9. **Discipline strategies.** This chapter discusses and explains how to implement a wide range of discipline strategies.

10. **Ages and stages.** This chapter describes how the meaning of children's behaviour is dependent upon the developmental phase in which the child is located, and how, during each phase, a child needs to master particular tasks.

11. **Communication skills.** This chapter looks at how to listen and the common pitfalls that parents can fall into.

12. **Stress management.** This chapter looks at how to manage stress for both parents and children, providing case studies.

The first eight chapters and Chapter 11 will help build the positive relationship between parents and their children, improving their child's self-esteem and ability to be socially competent, and with the chapters building upon each other. Chapter 9 gives parents a range of different discipline strategies for helping their children accept boundaries and behave appropriately. Chapter 10 gives parents fascinating information about how child development impacts on expectations of children's behaviour, and the role of the parent in helping children successfully master the skills necessary to develop through each stage.

Chapter 12 is a guide to understanding stress and the how to cope with difficult feelings so that relationships are not damaged by destructive behaviour.

I have used the real life experiences of families I have worked with to tell stories about the impact of implementing different parenting strategies. The case studies are an amalgam of different family experiences, and all details have been anonymized.

Chapter 1

Looking after Yourself

Looking after yourself is important because we need to feel positive about ourselves in order to look after our children. It is not selfish to get some of your own needs met; in fact it is essential. In this chapter we explore the reasons why this is vital, and also why our family patterns over previous generations could prevent us from being the parent we want to be.

Accepting that you can't be — and don't need to be — a perfect parent is a liberating feeling. To be 'good enough' is a major achievement! You can forgive yourself for being impatient sometimes, or for having the occasional takeaway meal instead of cooking. It can sometimes be enough that you have managed to get through the day without 'losing it' altogether.

As a parent you need to look after yourself. Imagine you are a jug full of all your emotional and physical resources. During the day you are using these up all the time with your children. Soon there will come a time when you have very few resources left. Therefore it is very important to have your own needs met too, in order to fill up your jug and have some emotional and physical energy left to give to your children. Look after yourself by meeting up with friends, getting enough sleep, watching football or your favourite TV programme, or doing whatever gives you joy. Asking for help from friends and relatives can also keep your jug full enough to cope with your children.

Our expectations of ourselves as parents are sometimes unrealistic and only end up leaving us feeling inadequate. Parents are supposed to be educators, cooks, cleaners, health and safety inspectors, counsellors, security guards, breadwinners, taxi drivers, fun to be with, clever, sympathetic and loving. To have all these attributes all the time is simply not realistic for one person.

These expectations put pressure on you as a parent, which only helps to leave you feeling more stressed with your children. Without these pressures, it can sometimes be much easier to be the parent that you want to be. We tend to see our children's behaviour as reflecting our competence as parents. This can lead to trying to control our children so much that they are not able to take responsibility for themselves. However, not letting children take responsibility for themselves can be risky. We can end up feeling exhausted but also the child does not have the opportunity to learn from experience and to develop self-confidence.

Our role changes from being 100 percent responsible when they are a baby to when they are aged 18, when hopefully, they can become independent, ready to start the process of leaving the family and taking much more responsibility for themselves. This is a massive change in a short space of time, and so parenting in many ways is about slowly letting go and giving our children all the skills they need for forming positive relationships and feeling they can make a difference in the world.

Looking at yourself as a parent and what you bring to the parent role can be useful in helping you understand what makes you tick and where your vulnerabilities are, what 'pushes your buttons' to leave you feeling furious or out of control. This self-understanding is important because it is a way of helping you look after yourself and not unwittingly sabotage yourself.

Parents who are able to understand and think about how they were parented, and why their parents behaved in that way (even if their experience of childhood was very difficult), will be much less likely to repeat a pattern of poor parenting. Your own childhood, and also the family patterns (scripts) from generations past, can give you interesting clues as to what might be being played out in your own life without you even realising it. These family patterns can be enormously powerful. Unless we address these unconscious patterns, it is easy to just follow them blindly.

Look at patterns in your family such as:

- relationships between mothers and fathers
- relationships between brothers and sisters
- relationships between parents and children
- the role of women and men
- how conflict is managed
- messages about sexuality
- effects of displacement from country of origin
- role of dominance and competition
- the intimacy or distance of relationships in the family.

By looking at your own family tree you can examine your possible blind spots and issues, so as not to repeat patterns unknowingly. If you have a partner it can be useful to explore how your family script could be very different to their family script. When you both have an understanding of each other's family patterns, then when problems flare up over child-rearing issues, you will be much better equipped to sort them out. This is because you will be able to see the issue from your partner's perspective as well, and hence find it easier to manage the difficulty.

The best way to understand how to do a family tree is to use an example to explain the principles.

Jenny and Pierre's Story

Jenny and Pierre had three children of their own, aged 10, 7 and 2. The eldest and youngest children were daughters. The middle child was a boy. Jenny also had a daughter from a previous relationship, Bella aged 14.

Pierre found parenting girls difficult. His father had left him when he was only eight years old, so he was having to create how to be a father without a model. He had been the eldest of four boys and had to take responsibility from a young age.

Jenny had a very acrimonious relationship with her mother who was an alcoholic. Jenny's grandmother was also a very angry woman who had been deserted by her husband and left to bring up two children on her own. There was no warmth in this relationship either.

Jenny and Pierre came to see me because they were having lots of problems with Jenny's 14 year old daughter, Bella. They felt like telling her to leave their home because she was being so rude and belligerent.

When we looked at their family tree together, we were able to see a pattern of very troubled relationships between daughters and mothers and very peripheral fathers. Jenny and Pierre decided to try and change their way of relating to the children so that Pierre got more involved. Jenny would try to do activities to bond with Bella, and to lower her expectations over behaviour. Jenny also became aware that she was showing favouritism to her son at the expense of her other daughters.

Pierre was able to see that he had high expectations of Bella because he had been so responsible and 'grown up' when he was 14. He realised that he found boys much easier to parent, as he had so much experience from his brothers. Pierre also became aware that his tendency to depression and distancing himself from his children could stem from his mother and grandmother both being depressed. He saw that he had to take care of himself, so as not to bring on any of his triggers for depression, such as stress, no exercise and not enough sleep.

By looking at their family tree they were able to start to examine their script and not pass it on unwittingly.

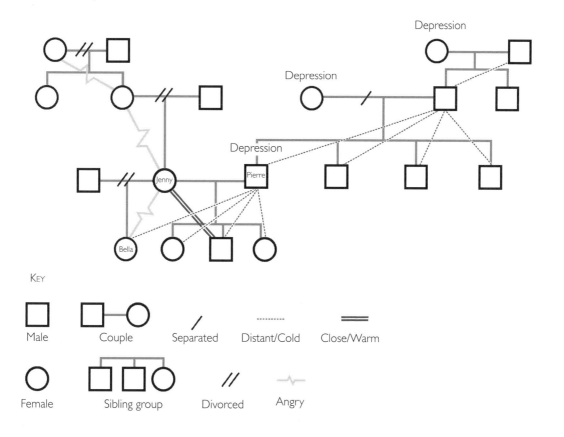

Figure 1: Jenny and Pierre's Family Story

EXERCISE

Try drawing your own family tree and then see if you can see any patterns in the closeness or distance of relationships that strike you. You can also label each person with any issues that might be in your family, such as depression, alcohol use, eating issues etc., and see if you can see any patterns emerging. Do the family tree with your partner or a friend and see if you can see any patterns going down through the generations. If they are good that's great; if you don't like them, think about this carefully and then whether it is possible not to repeat these patterns or scripts unconsciously.

David and Susan's Story

David and Susan came to see me because their 7 year-old son, Lucas, was violent and lacking in empathy, and seemed to take joy in hurting other children, including his brothers and sisters. In the first two sessions we looked at the family tree and what might be passed on from previous generations to Lucas. Susan had an older brother who had been violent and bullying towards her. He had an unfulfilled life with some of it spent in prison. Her father had also left home when she was 6 and she had not seen him again. Her maternal grandfather had been a violent alcoholic and she did not know her paternal grandfather. Susan had no positive male role models in her life as she was growing up.

David was a quiet unassuming man whose father was physically violent to him when he was growing up. He had vowed never to be like his father. His brother had also been violent and had mirrored his father, bullying his younger brother and sister. During these two sessions we were able to unpick that Susan unconsciously saw Lucas as her violent brother and was frightened of him, and that David also saw him as his father. We were able to work with these misconceptions to understand that Lucas was just a 7 year-old child and not his uncle or grandfather, but that he did need nurturing care and strong boundaries to feel safe. With support, David was able to become more authoritative in his parenting, and Susan was able to start child-led play with Lucas so that he stopped feeling so hated and hopeless. Lucas slowly became less aggressive, and the family managed to get back on an even keel.

Mandy and Kevin's Story

Mandy and Kevin came to see me because their marriage had become troubled since the birth of their daughter, Sarah. Kevin was a farmer and came from a farming family of many generations. Before they had Sarah, Mandy had an interesting and fulfilling job as a teacher and worked long hours. Kevin also worked long hours on the farm, rising early and coming home very late, especially in the Summer. Mandy felt isolated and overwhelmed now she was spending all her time on her own with Sarah. Kevin could not understand why Mandy was now being so demanding of him. He was also worried that he was not able to keep up with his work on the farm.

On exploring Kevin's family tree, it showed that his model of fathering was about being the breadwinner and working on the farm all the time. This was how both his father and grandfather had lived. We explored the fact that he did want to be a different type of father and more involved with his daughter, so he did not need to keep to these old family patterns.

Mandy had come from a family of teachers who had been perfectionists. She realised that she could become a little more relaxed, make sure she looked after her own needs by seeing friends and doing some exercise classes, and then she would not be so angry with Kevin when he returned from work.

By looking at their family tree, Kevin and Mandy were able to not repeat unhelpful patterns of relating and started to get on much better again.

Looking after Yourself: Key Points

★   Have realistic expectations of yourself as a parent.
★   Looking after yourself (both emotionally and physically) is not selfish but vital to ensure you are able to be the parent you want to be.
★   Look at your own family script for clues about the present.
★   Think about patterns you want to keep and those you want to discard.

Chapter 2

Feelings

This chapter explores the importance of acknowledging and accepting feelings to help children become aware of their own feelings. In this way they become able to recognize their feelings and then able to regulate them. It also looks at how we can express feelings so that they can be heard and not damage relationships.

Acknowledging and Accepting Feelings

Acknowledging our child's feelings is the best way to show that we understand and care about them. Sometimes it's not easy, however, as we can be confused by the strength of their feelings or by the seeming bizarreness of their reaction to a given event. However, by really observing our child and thinking about what is happening for them at that particular time, we can make an attempt to acknowledge the feeling. It is also sometimes useful to add a time reference to the acknowledgement, as the child can then appreciate that feelings can change – for example, 'this afternoon you're really furious at your sister because she's broken your lego palace'.

Some parents have not had a model of how to encourage their children to be sensitive, caring people by acknowledging their feelings. It can then be difficult to think about the long-term consequences of denying a child's feelings – that they may learn to hide their feelings, not trust them, or even learn not to feel at all. This could in turn influence their ability to think about how other people might be feeling, and hinder the development of empathy.

It is often enough to acknowledge the child's comment or feeling and reflect back that they have been heard – for example, 'I hate Abigail' could be acknowledged by 'It sounds like you really hate Abigail today'. Trying to find the correct word to convey to your child how they are feeling can be a challenge. Sometimes we can be puzzled as to why they seem to be so heartbroken that the biscuit is broken, or because we had to change our plans suddenly and not go to the park. However, by having the feeling acknowledged, the child feels understood and does not need to hold on to their upset. The following statements would therefore be helpful in these two scenarios: 'I know you're upset because the biscuit is broken' to the toddler, or 'I'm sorry you're disappointed that we can't go to the park', are statements that both show the child that you are trying to understand how they feel. It is important to remember that children have just as intense feelings as adults, even though we may think that their concerns are 'childish'.

Lewis and Maiya's Story

Lewis and Maiya came to me because their child was having trouble going to bed at night, saying that she had a tummy ache and could not go to sleep. Maiya had already checked out with her GP that her daughter was physically well. She thought about what might be going on for her daughter – perhaps not wanting to be separated from the rest of the family, and also that it was important to be empathic to her. She gave her daughter a special milky drink with some honey in it, and the child could tell that her feelings had been acknowledged and that her mother cared. She was then able to go to sleep.

Luke's Story

Luke's son thought that lions were asleep under his bed. Luke got an aerosol (saying that it had a special anti-lion smell) and sprayed deodorant under the bed to get rid of it. The child then felt safe to fall asleep.

In these two examples the parent is taking the child's worries seriously and using the parent's own imagination to think of solutions that not only acknowledge the child's feelings through words but also by actions. It is showing the child you are thinking about them and can put yourself in their shoes.

Sometimes just naming a feeling is enough. For example, Eve did not get the part in the school play that she wanted. Her mother was able to say to her, 'I can see you're really disappointed not to get the part you really wanted'. Her mother was tempted to say, 'but you got a smaller part which is fantastic', but she realised that Eve did not need this at the moment, as she was feeling disappointed. Reassuring her about the small part she'd been given would be denying her genuine feelings of disappointment.

If as parents we can give our children a large emotional vocabulary by putting their feelings into words, then they will not have to 'act out' their feelings but will be able to express them instead. Having a picture with lots of faces expressing different feelings can be a very helpful tool with young children for getting them thinking about feelings and the expressions that go with the feeling.

EXERCISE

Remember times as a child or teenager when you told your parents how you were feeling and were not acknowledged or were ignored with a response like 'Stop making a fuss'. What would you have liked to have heard and experienced instead? If you cannot remember back to your childhood, think of a more recent experience as an adult, perhaps asking for advice from a teacher or doctor, and not having your concerns acknowledged. How did you feel?

Research on the neuroscience of the brain has revealed fascinating information about how it regulates emotion. A way of understanding the brain which is useful when thinking about behaviour is to think of the brain as divided into three parts. First, there is **the brain stem** (the reptilian brain) which controls all the involuntary systems that keep you alive like breathing, and which includes the fight, flight, freeze automatic response to dangerous situations. Next there is **the limbic system** (the mammalian brain) which contains all the emotions and memories. **The pre-frontal cortex** (the human brain) controls language, abstract thought, complex decision making, planning, morality, imagination, empathy and reasoning.

When a child is having a major temper-tantrum the brain stem and limbic system have taken control. They flood the child's brain and body with the stress hormones adrenaline and cortisol. The effect of these hormones is to make the child go into an immediate stress response. Their pulse will go up, their hands will get sweaty, and they will feel hot. The child will have gone into a fight-flight-freeze-or-submit response. This is because this part of the brain does not have the capacity to regulate emotions, and the child will continue in fight, flight, freeze or submit mode. These hormones then take at least 20 minutes to be absorbed by the body and for the stress response to calm back down. Trying to talk rationally to the child would be pointless. It would only make things worse, while soothing the child and perhaps acknowledging feelings will help the pre-frontal cortex slowly to get involved and start to regulate the child's emotions.

Some children and young people who have very severe meltdowns and temper-tantrums could have had a difficult start to life. Through no fault of her own, perhaps, their mother was depressed and unable to respond to their demands and cues as babies. This would have caused the stress chemical cortisol to be constantly activated in the child's brain. Similarly, the child may have witnessed arguments and fights which scared them, or perhaps they had to go to hospital for procedures which they found frightening. Both of these experiences would have produced cortisol in their brain. When the child then has a mild frustration, they can go into total meltdown because the trigger for cortisol production has been activated, even though the mild frustration on its own would not have been enough. However, with lots of repetition of soothing responses, acknowledgement and special time (individual attention with the child in control of the play), children can become better able to regulate their emotions.

As an example, I was taking my 18-month old grandson home on the train which then stopped for a 45-minute delay. He was tired and hungry, and I had forgotten to bring any emergency supplies with me. He became very upset. I tried to soothe him by singing and acknowledging his feelings, but nothing worked. He cried louder and louder. Then a French lady came up to me and started to interact with him with an apple and a key ring playing a little game with him. Miraculously, this managed to help him soothe himself. After five minutes he had regained his emotional regulation and was able to manage the trip home. The French lady had been able to fire his curiosity which had in turn activated his pre-frontal cortex.

Mr Ahmed and Abdul's Story

I saw Mr Ahmed who had a child Abdul with autism. Abdul had completely lost control at a family party and had ended up screaming under the bed in his room. When we discussed the party, it became clear that Abdul was not clear what the routine was going to be and had not been prepared for all the noise and excitement. This had got too much for him, which had led to the total meltdown. Mr Ahmed realised that when an event was planned, Abdul had to be prepared very carefully to stop him going into a fear-or-flight response.

There is another type of temper-tantrum that parents know is more manipulative, because it is being controlled by the higher brain (the prefrontal cortex). This is obvious because when the child gets what they want, the tantrum stops.

Samantha and Paige's Story

Paige refused to eat the food that her mother had prepared for her, even though she eats the same food at school and at friends' houses. Paige's mother, Samantha, was at her wits' end, endlessly creating new meals for her daughter which were becoming more and more unhealthy. She would now only eat gravy with toast for dinner at home. When Samantha tried to be firm with Paige it was like 'World War 3'. She would scream for over four hours, with the result that Samantha gave into her.

Samantha had tried to use reasoning, rewards and incentives to help Paige, but these had been unsuccessful, perhaps because she thought they would not work and so had given up before they had a chance of being successful. The situation was getting so bad that Samantha felt she was hopeless as a mother.

With support Samantha regained her strength and was able to say to her daughter, 'I know you want toast and gravy but you can't have it. You can have the same meal that we're all eating. If you can't eat your dinner, I'll have to cancel your play date tomorrow because you'll be too hungry to enjoy it.' Paige responded very well to clear boundaries and respectful communication. In this example Paige was being manipulative because she stopped having a tantrum when she got the dinner she wanted (gravy and toast), and then when Samantha set clear boundaries she started to eat the normal meals that had been prepared for the family.

Some children are able to use their prefrontal cortex to regulate emotions in some places, such as at home, but they can find it very difficult at school if they are not the centre of attention all of the time, or are asked to do a challenging activity. In these cases, the feelings of shame, fear or sadness may loom so large for them that they become stressed, angry or uncontrollable. School staff would have to be very skilled at using soothing techniques to help the child be able to regulate himself again.

In my work as a family therapist I often see parents who tell me their child has no empathy for anyone else and is totally self-obsessed. This can be upsetting and frustrating for parents who are themselves very empathic towards other people. One of the often-ignored tasks of parenting is how to help build the child's capacity for empathy, for imagining how others feel apart from themselves.

Questions can be very useful for developing this capacity.

- **Why do you think the little girl felt sad?** (when you see a child crying after being told off)
- **Why do you think that lady was so brisk with me?**
- **Why do you think that toddler was laughing so much?**
- **What do you think your friend Keith feels about moving school?**
- **I know you want to win very much, but how do you think the children who don't come first feel?**

This type of questioning can help build up empathy for other people in a natural way. Helping children to understand their own feelings can also be very important in generating self-understanding.

Mrs Grant and Anna's Story

Mrs Grant came to see me because she was going into hospital for an operation. She was very worried about her daughter Anna, who was very clingy and hated being separated from her. She was concerned that Anna might be even more upset when she was in hospital. I asked both Mrs Grant and Anna to draw pictures of all their worries, and also to draw what they would like to happen in order to feel better. With these drawings Anna was able to explore her feelings to gain some more self-awareness about her anxiety. Mrs Grant and Anna were then able to plan positively for managing during the hospital admission.

Expressing Our Feelings

How we express ourselves is very important in helping children to be able to listen to our requests. Sometimes we make the mistake of thinking that our children or people close to us are telepathic, that they know exactly what we feel without being told. Some people are gifted with the ability to read body language very accurately, but these are very much in the minority. In order to help our children accept our feelings it is important to state clearly what we feel, think or want. We need to own these for ourselves by using 'I' statements rather than 'you'.

It is also important not to be blaming, and to describe the behaviour and not the person – for example, 'You've dropped the banana on the carpet and it's been trodden in', rather than 'You're a very messy child!'.

A useful concept in thinking about how to express feelings is thinking of yourself as a thermometer! If you feel that you are boiling over with an emotion at 100 degrees, it is best not to express your feelings because you may end up shouting. This will only make the situation much worse. When your 'thermometer' is midway at 50 degrees – when your emotions are more under control – then you can express your feelings calmly without the risk of losing your temper.

A mantra that many parents find useful when they want to express a feeling to their child is the 'Four-Part Statement':

- I feel …
- When you …
- Because …
- How can you help me with this problem?

With very young children it helps to put the last statement first:

- Help, I have a problem
- I feel …
- When you …
- Because …
- How can you help me with this?

Vanessa's Story

Vanessa told me she had used this statement with her three young boys when they walked into her kitchen with their boots on, leaving mud all over the floor. She said:
'Help, I have this big problem.
I feel … upset
when … you don't take your boots off,
because … then I have to clean the kitchen floor again.
How can you help me with this?'

The three little boys then thought together, got a brush, pan and cloth and started to clean up after themselves. Vanessa was thrilled!

Seema's Story

Seema used the Four-Part Statement to express how upset she was with the untidiness of her teenagers' rooms. She said:
'I feel cross … when you leave your clothes on the floor.
Because …then they need to be washed and ironed again.
How can you help me with this?'
The children started to put their clothes on hangers.

EXERCISE

Think of a behaviour that your child does that annoys you. Devise a 'Four-part Statement' to tell them. Hopefully you should get a positive result from this so that the child will change that behaviour.

We often unwittingly treat our children as mind-readers. When we actually say how we feel about something, and the reason for this, our children are then enabled to make positive choices so as to make things better. It gives children great opportunities for developing problem-solving skills. It increases their self-esteem because they are sorting out problems on their own.

Sometimes their solution may not be what you had in mind. For example, when my daughter was 3 years old, she demonstrated to me the power of letting children sort out solutions for themselves. Jess was running to the park too quickly, ahead of her friends. I said, 'I feel worried when you run ahead because I need to keep you all together. How can you help me with this problem?' Jess thought for a while, then took her boots off and put the right boot on the left foot and vice versa. 'Now I can go slower', she said.

Stating the Positive

One way to encourage our children to avoid mistakes, accidents and unacceptable behaviour is to try to avoid the word 'don't' and put statements into a positive idiom.

'Close Your Eyes and Don't Think about Snow'

What came into your head when you thought about that statement? I am sure you thought about snow, and even got a picture of snow in your mind. Now imagine what would happen if you said to your child, 'Don't drop the milk …' 'Don't touch the TV …' 'Don't be naughty …' 'Don't run on the grass …'.

When we say 'don't,' we risk encouraging our children to think about what we least want them to do. When we ask a question or make a statement, the hearer has to think about our words to make sense of them. So even as we make a negative statement, we run the risk of encouraging just what we want to avoid – by inviting them to think about it. The 'don't' can get lost. So then the child can even be left with a strong command to do the exact opposite of what you're wanting!

If you make statements in a positive way, it is much more likely that your child will behave appropriately. For example, 'Hold the glass of milk with two hands, please … Show me the toy rabbit … Show your teacher your careful work … Stay on the path, please'.

From my own experience, I can remember being on a walk with my sister and having a very narrow stream to jump over. My sister said 'don't fall into the water', and I immediately jumped straight into the stream!

Feelings: Key Points

★　Accept and acknowledge feelings by stating what you think the child is feeling.
★　Express your feelings using the Four-part Statement: I feel … when you … because … and then you can ask for help to sort it out if appropriate.
★　Put commands into the positive and avoid using the word 'don't'.

Chapter 3

Child-led Play

This chapter describes the importance of play for a child's development and then continues to describe a very special form of that play a parent can engage in with their child, called Child-led Play (sometimes also known as Special Time). It is a unique experience shared by one parent and one child. It helps to develop a close relationship between them.

Children develop through playing. They learn how to make relationships, how to share, stand up for themselves and to negotiate. They discover about the difference between fantasy and reality, and are able to play with these concepts. My grandson asked me on the way to the playground if the playground was in the sky. We had a long conversation about what it would be like if the playground was in the sky, and he suggested ideas like 'it could fall down' or 'it would be difficult to get to' – and he was excited to play with these ideas. Play is the way children learn to think. Through play children develop their creativity, spontaneity, sense of humour, desire to communicate and imagination. A walk in the park can become an adventure where anything is possible.

Play helps children make sense of their thoughts and feelings so that a child who is going to hospital may spend weeks after their return re-enacting the experiences of having a bandage on their arm by playing hospitals with their teddies and wrapping bandages around their arms. As parents it is useful to prepare children for new experiences with play. Thus if your child is starting school you could play 'going to school' or read books together about starting school. This helps reduce the fear of new experiences.

Fatima and Aisha's Story

Fatima came to see me to ask for help for her 8 year old daughter Aisha because she was bedwetting and not doing well at school. She told me that her husband and her had a very acrimonious divorce and that the contact arrangements were very tense, with Aisha crying and not wanting to stay at her father's but being fine when she got there. I worked with both the parents to help them put Aisha's needs first and sort out contact arrangements which did not upset her.

However, I also worked individually with Aisha. She would come into the room and straight away put on Cindrella clothes from my dressing-up clothes rail. She would then spend the rest of the session acting out different plots around how badly Cindrella was being treated and how she had no power to influence what was happening to her. Through these sessions she was able to think about her experience with her parents and it enabled her to be more assertive in stating her needs. She stopped wetting the bed, and started to do better at school.

A child's world is in the present – they may want to spend 30 minutes looking at a beetle or examining a weed. They can concentrate for long periods on an object that has caught their imagination.

Play is vital for a child's healthy development; both play with a parent and playing in groups or by oneself give children the opportunity to experience the world in different ways and to develop their individuality. However, the most important aspect about play is that it is fun. Without play the world would be a sad place.

Having a box of play resources for your child can give endless amounts of fun for her. Items can be paints, crayons, felt tips, cutting and sticking material, play dough, dressing-up clothes, cars and garages, lego and duplo bricks, wooden train sets, small people and creatures, farm and wild animals, dolls, teddies and puppets. I find going to charity shops a brilliant resource of toys without having to spend much money. A washing-up bowel of water with some cups and a jug, or a sheet placed over a couple of chairs making a tent, can both keep a toddler or pre-school child busy for ages. Making a shop or doing pretend cooking with items from your kitchen cupboards and saucepans can help let your child's imagination run wild. Having toys in the bath such as ducks, a sponge, a jug, beakers etc. can also make bath time a great playtime experience as well as one for getting clean!

As children get older, board games and cards become more interesting as children enjoy rule-bound games. Computer games also become more interesting to children and teenagers, but parental guidance needs to be maintained to ensure that the young person is not on screen for too long to the detriment of other areas of their development.

More Thoughts on Computer Games

I have had many parents coming to see me concerned and confused about their children's gaming. When they ask their children to come off the screen they are met with huge tantrums and defiance. I am concerned that children's brain development is fragile. The neural pathways that make up the brain are being laid down all the time from the experiences the child has. By giving children computers too early, they can get addicted to games which only stimulate sight and sound. They are not experiencing movement, physical touch, taste, smell. Since the beginning of time children have played with objects and been in communication with other children and adults in order to grow in a healthy way. Relationships are complicated, and it is only by repetition of interactions that you learn to pick up social cues and get an idea of who you are in the world.

The problem with computers is that they can be very seductive to parents as they are great babysitters. However, I would like to caution parents against too much screen time with very young children as they need to learn with all their senses. Also, for young children the difference between reality and fantasy is a very thin line. By adding another dimension of a virtual world, you could be adding yet another layer of confusion for the child.

Child-Led Play and Special Time

Letting your child take the lead gives them an experience of being in control and safely taking responsibility in a situation they enjoy. Having Special Time with your child will be enormously beneficial in building up a strong relationship. Your child will benefit from your undivided attention (even 10 minutes a day can reap huge rewards), and allowing your child to show you how they play will help you enjoy their company more. It may even encourage your own creativity to flourish. The child feels they are being truly witnessed, which is enormously good for increasing their self-esteem.

The key points of Special Time are:

- It is non-directive – follow the child's lead; avoid telling them what to do.
- Play for a limited time (it is actually hard to give 100 percent concentrated attention to a child for more than 10 minutes, at least at first.) You might want to make it longer but be careful because you don't want it to become a chore.
- It is different from other types of play.
- Set up rules beforehand – for example, they cannot hurt anyone or damage anything.
- Your child is otherwise in total control.
- It is not 'educational'; they will learn, but you are not teaching.
- Don't make interpretations – you might think the child is drawing a tree, but if you say 'you are drawing a tree' you could unwittingly take over because your child was really drawing a giant, for example.
- No questions or talking apart from descriptive commenting – for example, 'you're drawing a long line, you're using the blue pencil very carefully'.
- Do Special Time with your child three times a week if possible, even if the child has been badly behaved that day. Special Time is about building your relationship.
- After 10 minutes play, tell your child you have to stop now, saying something like, '10.9.8.7.6.5.4.3.2.1 blast-off!'. Tell your child that you have to do something else now. They can stay playing, but you will not be with him any longer this time.

Patrick and Ellen's Story

Patrick and Ellen were totally exhausted by their daughter Amy who fought with her brother all the time. Nothing seemed to keep her happy, however much they tried. Both Patrick and Ellen had full-time jobs which involved some overnight visits away from home. Amy and her brother were sometimes looked after by their grandmother. They also went to breakfast club and afternoon club, which they loved.

When Patrick and Ellen started doing Special Time, they both decided to do it with each child every day, alternating which child they did it with. Amy adored this time, and spent it making complicated pictures and constructions with junk modelling. She called it 'Blast-off' time. After a couple of weeks, Amy's behaviour changed. She was no longer the needy child who could never get enough attention, but was happy playing with her brother, and loving towards her parents.

It is best to avoid playing a competitive game with younger children because this could be difficult to manage if the child does not win. Special Time is about building attachment, not the importance of adhering to rules, so the time could get spoilt this way. Unstructured play with toys, dolls and blocks are great because they have no end-product. Creative activities are especially useful and great fun – for example, clay, play dough, and cutting and sticking.

When children have experienced child-led play, they often develop a long concentration span so they are then able to entertain themselves with their toys for quite long periods after their parent has finished playing with them, only needing the occasional acknowledgement to happily continue playing using their own imagination.

Some parents find it helpful to have Special Time at the same time each day. Switching the phone off helps children know that the time you are spending together is important. Special Time is about building up an individual bond, and it is really important to do it with just one child at a time, which may require careful planning. Try to play with each child separately at first, if possible. Give descriptive comments while the child is playing, a bit like a football commentary. Some children like to have the descriptive commentary all the time whilst others are happy just with the odd word here and there.

Special Time is about totally accepting your child, because they are so often told what to do. This is a small amount of time when they are in charge. The secret of Special Time is that you are giving 100 percent attention, and children thrive on a parent's attention.

Some children can be quite bewildered if they are asked to choose what they would like to play with. For these children it can be useful to start with three different things they could do, such as cutting and sticking, playing with the lego, or playdough. Once they get the idea that they can do whatever they want, they will start to be able to make their own decisions and get very excited about this opportunity. Sometimes it can be useful to observe your child playing when you are not playing with them; from this you can learn what type of play they are interested in, and in turn this could give you ideas from which to choose the three alternatives to offer for Special Time.

An extension of Special Time can be a day out, with the child doing whatever they want to do. My mother would do this with all her grandchildren, taking them to the zoo, museums, swimming, the park or to the cinema. They all adored this and developed a very close bond with their grandmother.

Special Time with a Baby or Toddler

When you have Special Time with a baby or toddler, it comes much more naturally. In some ways you are creating a space for them in which to play where they feel completely secure to explore the world and their surroundings. For babies, a parent's body is the best play-thing. Just follow the child's lead and comment on what they are experiencing – for example, 'I can see you love having that fluffy teddy to suck...You are so interested in that other baby that you want to stroke her face'.

I look after my own grandson one day a week. His favourite game is called 'Where's Harry?' where he looks through a nylon tunnel while I call 'Where's Harry?'. He crawls down the tunnel and I say 'Harry's crawling down the tunnel'; then I go to the other end and call 'Where's Harry?' again – at which point he turns round and comes to me from that side. All I am doing is describing his behaviour, yet he loves the game and could play it all day.

Treasure Baskets

Babies also love treasure baskets, a play activity developed by Elinor Goldschmied (1994) in a book called *People under three: Young children in day care* to encourage exploration and curiosity in babies. The baby's brain is growing very quickly as it responds to streams of stimulation coming from its six senses, sight, touch, smell, hearing, taste and bodily movement. You can give the child a basket of objects to play with that they can explore with all these senses. The objects can be chosen that offer interest in each of these areas. You can adapt this to do special time with your baby for 10 minutes while he is playing with the objects by giving attention and describing what your baby is doing as he sits beside the basket: for example, 'Now you are touching the fir cone and putting it in the eggcup', or 'You are banging the rattle very hard on the floor and making a loud noise'.

Resources that Elinor Goldschmied recommended in her book are some of the following, but you can also have fun using your own creativity, or in having different themes.

Fir cones, differing sizes , big feathers, dried gourds, a lemon, an apple, large corks, large shells, woollen ball, little baskets, tooth brush, cosmetic brush, wooden nail brush, small boxes, rattles of various types, clothes peg, coloured beads on string, wooden bricks, cylinders, cotton reel, ring, spoon, egg cup, spoons, small egg-whisk, bunch of keys, lemon squeezer, key rings linked together, metal egg cup, tea strainer, bicycle bell, small saucepans, leather purse, coloured marble eggs, high bouncer ball, velvet powder puff, small rag doll, tennis ball, spectacle case, bath plug and chain, small teddy bear, bean bag, small cloth bag containing lavender, rosemary, thyme, cloves, greaseproof paper, tinfoil, small cardboard boxes, inside of kitchen paper rolls.

EXERCISE

Think about what might get in the way of incorporating Special Time into your daily routine, and what you could do to overcome that?

Parents with whom I work will often say at first that Special Time is boring; that they don't have enough time; that there are so many distractions all the time, or that they don't know how to play, saying they feel uncomfortable or embarrassed to try because it looks silly. Once they start incorporating Special Time into their routine, however, they start to really enjoy the experience.

Deborah and Callum's Story

Deborah came to me furious with her child Callum because he didn't listen to her, and seemed wilfully disobedient. We spoke about starting to do Special Time because they seemed to have so few positive times together. Deborah had been brought up in care with no memory of playing with any caring adult when she was growing up. Deborah and I worked together to help her be able to play with Callum in a nurturing way, letting him take the lead and following his signals.

The first few times I met with Deborah, we practised doing Special Time and talked about the importance of being creative, being witnessed, and being helped to feel special. Deborah was able to bring Callum to the next sessions and do Special Time with him, with a little support from me. She then began doing it at home with Callum, finding that she really started to value spending this very enjoyable time with him. As a result of the improvement in their relationship, Callum started to behave much better.

The Bottomless Bucket

Some parents say that their child seems like a bottomless bucket – that they give and give and give and it is never enough. Then they start to feel exhausted and resentful.

Gillian and Emma's Story

Gillian felt totally fed up with her daughter Emma, who could never get enough of her undivided attention. For example, she had taken Emma out for the day: they had been on the beach, had a picnic, then gone to see a film and had pizza and ice cream before coming home. Her daughter had been exhausted but happy and the day had gone well. Then at bedtime, Emma had a massive temper tantrum, saying the day was a disaster because her favourite pyjamas were in the wash. Gillian felt like giving up. We spoke about how some children – for whatever reason – have such fragile self-esteem that it is as if all the good things you do with the child seem pointless, because it is never enough.

It is useful to think of these children as a bucket with a hole in it, so that all the good experiences seem to disappear and they never seem to have enough of them. These children often just need a lot of proof that you do really care for them. You need to fill the bucket up with glue (lots of attention, love and special time), and then finally the hole will seal – their bucket will be full. The important lesson is to not give up, and for yourself not to get too emotionally upset.

Parents often don't realise that their child is not just being selfish and demanding in these situations, but is acting out their need to feel that they are unconditionally loved. It's often helpful to think about how the things you do together can give them this feeling.

Child-led Play: Key Points

1. Children develop and learn through playing.
2. Through play children develop their creativity, spontaneity, sense of humour, desire to communicate and imagination.
3. Play helps children to understand and manage their feelings and thoughts.

Child-led Play

Spending 10 minutes a day with your child doing child-led play can give enormous positive benefits to your relationship.

★ Follow the child's lead.
★ Let the child decide what they want to do with the 10 minutes.
★ Do a descriptive commentary of what the child is doing (some children need a lot, others just need the odd comment).
★ Do not ask questions.
★ Do not make judgements (praise or put-downs).
★ No interpretations of what the child is doing.
★ At the end of 10 minutes, do a count-down (10 to 1 with 'blast off' at the end) to finish the session, but let the child continue without you if they want to. You can also do a one-minute signal before the end.
★ Even if the child has been badly behaved during the day, it is important keep child-led play and still give them the 10 minutes of Special Time. The child-led play should not be dependent on their good behaviour.

Chapter 4

Parenting Styles

Parenting styles are important to reflect upon as we parent are children. This is because they deeply influence the quality of the relationships that we will develop with our children.

There are three main parenting styles:

1.   aggressive
2.   permissive
3.   assertive

Most of us use a mixture of all three, with our style influenced by how we were parented ourselves. A parent may decide that they want to do everything differently to how they were brought up. When under stress, though, the way we were parented can come to dominate, even if we don't want it to. Consider how many times we think, 'I sound just like my father/mother'. Sometimes we have different parenting styles for different children, depending on their temperament, gender or position in the family. It's no surprise that this can cause conflict.

The Aggressive Parent Is Authoritarian

Aggressive parents use power, force and control to get children to behave in the way they want them to. They give a strong message of 'Do as you're told and don't question it'. Children may feel fearful of them. Such a parent will want all decisions to go their way. Children are not encouraged to have their own opinions, but to do as they're told without thinking. Children of these parents may not have much idea of how to take responsibility for themselves.

When children are young, this may produce very 'good' obedient behaviour, but as they become teenagers they will want more independence. Problems may then emerge in the relationships. There are two types of response that a child or teenager might make to an aggressive parent:

- The children or teenagers could become rebels and fight their parents by disobeying them. They might feel unloved and furious. They may also become hardened, say they hate their parent, and pretend not to care.

- Some children or teenagers will retreat, give up, and withdraw into themselves, just submitting to whatever their parent suggests. They learn to give in straight away at any sign of conflict, and will tend to have very low self-esteem. For their adult life this could cause problems, as they will not feel able to ask directly for their needs to be met.

James and Erica's Story

James and Erica came to see me because their 15 year-old son was saying he would prefer to live in a ditch rather than ever be in the same house as his father.

Erica was devastated because she was caught in the middle between her husband and son fighting – loving them both but feeling hopeless in the face of all this hatred. James felt that their son Tom 'was getting away with murder', treating the house like a hotel, not doing his school work properly, and not sharing in family time with his younger sister but disappearing into his room.

James had a very strict upbringing and left home at 16 to join the army. In two family therapy sessions we explored James's experiences of being fathered and how parenting styles needed to change as children grow up. I was able to tell James that Tom's rebellious behavior was similar to James's experience of growing up, that Tom was being 'a chip off the old block', and that he was growing up to be an independent young man. James later told me that this enabled him to feel that he was not 'giving in' or letting Tom walk all over him if he did start doing some negotiation. This enabled James and his son to develop a new relationship based on a more assertive style of parenting, and not the authoritarian type that proved so ineffective with a strong-minded teenager.

Holly and Esme's Story

Holly was furious with her daughter Esme and ended up screaming at her all the time, especially when she tried to get her out of the house to go to school.

In my sessions with Holly we spent a lot of time practising and learning about communication styles. Holly started to develop a less confrontational style of communication and Esme's level of aggression then lessened considerably. Holly reported that Esme was much better behaved now, giving an example of when Esme hadn't wanted to go to school and was having a tantrum about leaving the house because her shoes were too tight. Holly was able to stay calm (Esme had worn those shoes comfortably for the last three months). She just said, 'It is so annoying when you feel your shoes are too tight', whereas normally she would have said, 'Stop being so difficult and selfish, you are making us all late', which would have made the situation worse.

The Permissive Parenting Style Is Passive and Weak

They let children walk all over them and find it difficult to create boundaries. Parents with this approach can seem very loving and caring on the surface. However, because they are giving in all the time, the child will get more and more selfish, taking everything for granted, and unconsciously resenting their parents for not standing up for themselves. They will push the parents further and further to stand up for themselves.

These children will probably not be popular at school because they will not have learnt the important lessons of how to manage if you don't always get your own way. Parents who are very passive may sometimes explode when they feel they have been taken advantage of too much, losing their temper completely and then feeling guilty afterwards – making amends or giving in to their child – so that the cycle will repeat again and again.

Sometime parents who have had very aggressive parenting themselves say that they want to be completely different from their parents. They develop a permissive approach but then find that they're losing their temper all the time because they don't feel respected.

Petra and Sophia's Story

Petra was a lone parent with a seven year-old daughter she was finding impossible to control. She had experienced very aggressive parenting herself, often being beaten, and had vowed never to be like her parents. She had unwittingly developed a very permissive style of parenting. Sophia would not do anything she was told and just ignored Petra's requests, whether it was to go to bed now or to eat her dinner. Petra was at the end of her tether, and the relationship was not good for either of them. Petra was exhausted, she had no support from Sophia's father, her parents were estranged, and she had no network of friends around her. Her own self-esteem was low, so she found it very hard to set limits for Sophia because then she would have to withstand Sophia's anger.

I saw Petra for six sessions, and she began to see that she had to look after her own needs first so that she could parent Sophia. She started doing a few things for herself and managed to get a babysitter so she could go out one evening a week. We worked on how to do Special Time and to devise a list of household rules that she thought important enough to insist upon.

Petra then started doing Special Time with her daughter every day, but at the same time she also started to stand much firmer on her boundaries. Things slowly started to improve at home, and both Sophia and Petra became a lot happier. The quality of their relationship improved dramatically so that they enjoyed being in each other's company.

The Assertive Parent Knows when to Say 'No', which Creates Safe Boundaries for Their children

Assertive parents help their children solve problems and know how to listen to them. They are straightforward with their children, treat them with respect, and are respected themselves. These parents are fair and teach their children their own values and beliefs. Children with parents who are assertive will have better self-worth and an ability to relate well to other people because they respect their needs and feelings.

Other Parenting Styles

Manipulative Parenting Style
This type of parenting is passive-aggressive, using guilt and emotional blackmail to try to make the child comply – for example, 'Go to bed now, as I have an awful headache', or 'If it hadn't been for you, I could have been a famous singer, so don't make a fuss'.

Over-indulgent Parenting Style
Sometimes parents feel guilty if they have to work long hours or do not have the ideal home circumstances. They can then find it difficult to set boundaries so that their children learn to manipulate them by inducing guilt feelings in them. They may also throw money at their children – for example, buying presents or sweets because they want their child to like them, but not doing the hard work of spending time developing a relationship.

Over-protective Parenting Style

Parents may be over-protective because of issues from their own past. This means their children may become scared of the outside world, or go to the other extreme and start taking big risks because they've had little exposure to it.

Demanding Parenting Style

These parents are never happy with their children, believing they never work hard enough, achieve good-enough marks, or behave as the parents would like. These children could become very disheartened, give up and never feel that they're worthwhile. They could also become perfectionists but take no joy in their achievements.

Think of the style you most often use in your parenting and the effect it has on your child or teenager. Draw a circle and make 'cake slices' in it to illustrate the proportion of different types of parenting style you use. Think about whether it differs for different children.

Parenting Styles: Key Points

There are three main types of parenting style as well as some subsidiary ones.
We all do a little of all of them, but it is helpful to be aware of what they all are and if we are tending too much to use an unhelpful parenting style.

★ Aggressive parenting leading to unhappy children who can become aggressive themselves, angry, rebellious, scared or shut down.

★ Permissive parenting leading to unhappy children who may feel uncared for, scared, too powerful, and who find it difficult to fit into friendship groups.

★ Assertive parenting leading to a happy child secure in their environment, able to meet their needs and express their feelings, and let other people also have their needs met.

★ Manipulative parenting that leads to confused unhappy children who have been on the receiving end of emotional blackmail, but are not quite able to work out how they feel.

★ Over-indulgent/guilty parenting leads to children who can become manipulative themselves as they can see their parents' weak spots.

★ Over-protective parenting can lead to children who are anxious and scared, or who may become risk-takers.

★ Demanding parenting can lead to children feeling they can never be good enough and wanting to give up trying.

Chapter 5

Descriptive Praise

Descriptive praise is when you specifically praise your child's behaviour, instead of saying something general like, 'Well done' or 'good girl'. It can be like a magic wand for changing children's behaviour to be more positive. This praise makes a child feel valued and more likely to repeat the behaviour that brought the praise. It is a valuable positive parenting strategy to help children learn to behave appropriately.

Descriptive praise conveys acceptance, and enhances self-esteem and confidence. It can be even more effective when you add the effect and how you feel about it. These are the three components of descriptive praise:

- Describe the behaviour – be specific, so they know what they have done
- State the effect, if there is one
- Say how you feel about it
- 'I really liked the way you stayed out of your brother's way, even though he was trying to wind you up. That took a lot of will power – I was impressed.'

Praise should be used carefully, however, as it can seem ridiculous if you know that the behaviour doesn't warrant it.

Fiona's Story

Fiona recounted how she had started using descriptive praise with her son. He came home from school with a cake that he'd made in home economics. She said that it was really light and tasty, and beautifully decorated.

Her son was delighted. She asked what gave him the idea to add all the finishing touches, and he said, 'because I am a cook'. Descriptive praise is empowering because it gives children the ability to praise themselves.

Descriptive praise enhances the child's self-esteem. It develops their feeling of being in control of their own lives, freeing them from dependence on other people's view of them to feel good about themselves. This is especially important when the child reaches adolescence and peer pressure is much stronger. With general praise – for example, 'good work' – the child is being 'assessed' by the other person, and so develops what is termed an 'external locus of evaluation'. Their good feelings about themselves will be dependent on what someone else thinks about them.

Descriptive praise shows how much notice you're really taking, by commenting on details. It enhances self-confidence, self-sufficiency and independence. It means that the child will take satisfaction in their achievements.

When giving praise, it is important not to have any negative, conditional elements tacked on, or the praise will be received as a put down – for example, 'Thank you for cleaning up your bedroom, pity you don't do it more often', or 'You can be really good at spelling, when you put your mind to it'. Children will only hear the negative comment.

Margaret and Abi's Story

Margaret found it very hard to praise her teenage daughter because they'd had so many conflicts.

Abi's school had sent a very complimentary email to Margaret about what an enormous help she had been at the open evening for maths. However, Margaret had just caught her daughter smoking. She felt disappointed and frustrated, and could not make herself give Abi any praise for getting such a positive message from school. Abi was furious with her mother. It took a few sessions to help Margaret see the benefits of praise to encourage positive behaviour. Margaret had not been praised by her parents when she was a child, and so found it difficult to give praise, as she thought that her daughter should behave in a responsible way without the need for praise.

Making Praise More Powerful

Praise can be even more powerful if it is overheard by the child – for example, if the parent tells the grandparent some accomplishment the child did while the child is listening, such as, 'Did you know that Arthur can put all his clothes on by himself?'. For a young child it is more powerful to praise straight away rather than waiting a couple of hours when the child may have forgotten what they did.

Showing Your Love

Sometimes we can tell our child that they are important and unique because they exist. It does not need to be tied to any behaviour, but lets the child know that they're special and very much loved – for example, 'I love you because you are you'.

Children who Find It Difficult to Receive Praise

Some children find it difficult to receive praise for various reasons. Sometimes they feel they don't deserve it. Parents can get very frustrated with these children because their praise gets rejected, so they stop wanting to give it. However, these children need praise as much as any other. Giving praise more indirectly can be the answer with such children. When the child is barely aware of it, you can say 'Oh, that looks like an interesting picture', or 'You've been concentrating on that piece of writing a long time', with perhaps a slight touch on the shoulder as you go past. The child might not acknowledge the praise explicitly but can absorb that it has been given.

Another interesting side-effect of descriptively praising your child is that they may start descriptively praising their friends – for example, the child saying to their friend, 'I thought you did a great shot into the goal'. This is a way of helping friendship-building with their peers.

EXERCISE

Think of three things you do and praise yourself for it, such as, 'I'm doing my best as a parent even when things are tough ... I read a story to my child every night'.

Parents often undervalue themselves, thinking that they're not being good enough, but sometimes we need to praise ourselves for just keeping on going!

EXAMPLES

Getting Ready in the Morning
- You got out of bed and brushed your teeth and put your clothes on without me. That was very helpful.
- You've got your socks on all by yourself.
- You were kind to your sister when she spilt the milk by helping her mop it up.
- Thank you for getting your own breakfast cereal. That shows self-reliance.

Mealtimes

- Thank you for staying at the table until we all finish.
- It's nice to sit and have dinner with you.
- I'm glad you had some of the chicken.
- Thanks for putting your plate in the sink.

Bedtime

- Thank you for going to bed when I asked you first time.
- You only got out of bed twice last night. And each time I took you back to bed you were fine.
- You're in your pyjamas, even though you wish you could stay up later.

Teenagers

- Thanks for ringing to tell me you'll be home late. I won't worry now.
- I appreciate you left the party before your friends did. It must have been tempting to stay.

Helping about the House

- You hung your school clothes up when you got back from school.
- I'm glad you wiped your feet on the mat on your way in.
- You have done a careful job of putting those fragile toys away.
- You were a big help to me when you played with the baby while I put the shopping away.
- Thank you for waiting patiently while I was reading to your sister.

Descriptive Praise: Key Points

★ Describe what the child did, and if appropriate say how you felt about it and its effect.

★ Avoid put-downs or conditional praise.

★ Praising descriptively gives a child an internal locus of evaluation so they are not dependent on others to feel good.

★ Even children who brush aside descriptive praise will appreciate it.

★ Overheard praise can be very powerful.

Chapter 6

Labels

The purpose of this chapter is to explain the crippling effect that labels can have on children by stopping them developing their full potential. It then explains how parents can describe the behaviour instead of giving the child a label.

Labels can be like a self-fulfilling prophecy and stick with you throughout your life. If a child is told enough times that they're not bright, are just like their father (who was bad news), or will come to no good, this is often what happens.

Labels are very interesting for how they apply in families. A label can become a role. One child may have a label of 'the clever one', one 'the practical one', or 'the pretty one'. These labels can end up forcing a child into that role. The best way to try to change this is to deliberately do the opposite of what they might expect – for example, asking the child you think is untidy to help to sort out the kitchen cupboards, or asking the 'unreliable' child to fetch milk and bread from the local shop.

Some parents ask me what is so wrong with having a positive label such as 'helpful', for instance; but such a label could define a child who may not want to be helpful all the time, but sometimes want to be single-minded and finish their own project.

Labelling is related to our perceptions and filters towards our child. These play a crucial role in influencing how we see people. Perception and filters are the emotional attitudes towards our child which form the basis from which we view their behaviour. A simple example of when we're influenced in this way is if we are told something negative or positive about someone before we meet them. In my experience, this can completely or largely determine how I see the person at our first meeting. I need to meet them a few more times before I can form my own opinion without the effect of the information received before I met them.

EXERCISE

Think of one of your children and get a picture or a sense of him or her in your mind. Keep that picture constant, looking at it with the attitude of: 'My child is like a bottomless pit, demanding from me all the time.' Be aware of your feelings towards your child.

Keep the same picture in your mind and look at it with the attitude of, 'My child is difficult and intentionally naughty to upset me'. Be aware of your feelings again – have they changed?

Now imagine your child with the attitude of, 'My child is totally loveable'. How does this internal attitude change the way you feel about your child? Did the label affect how you saw them?

With some children who can sometimes be very difficult, it can be helpful to put pictures of your child being really gorgeous around your bedroom so that you have that internal memory of your child being really lovable.

Dagmar's Story

Dagmar came to see me because her 'devil child' would never do what he was told. By the age of six he'd already been expelled from three schools. He was violent and aggressive towards his little brother, to children at school, and also to his mother. His father saw him at weekends and mid-week and also said he was a 'devil child'. The child's reputation followed him wherever he went.

After an assessment, it was found that Dagmar's son had complex psychological difficulties. Once we'd set up a proper plan that included child psychotherapy, parenting classes for his parents as well as some couple work with both of them, they were able to parent him more appropriately. They understood the triggers for his aggressive behaviour and he was able to settle in to a very well-structured school and to thrive. He no longer had to live up to his label.

As parents, we sometimes label our child as naughty, clumsy, shy, and so on. These labels can 'stick', so describing the behaviour rather than the child is a more useful way of giving them the message that they can change. It prevents the child having a label hanging round their neck, limiting their potential.

The label 'naughty', which covers all sorts of behaviour, could be changed from 'you naughty child' to 'when you hit your brother it was unkind', or 'when you copied Karen's homework it didn't help you learning about fractions'.

The label 'clumsy' could be changed to 'You knocked over the jug when you rushed to get your plate'.

The label 'shy' could be changed to 'It takes you time to feel at ease with new people'.

Although it can feel awkward at first to describe the behaviour and not just give a label, it's much more helpful in the long term, as the child then has options about how to behave and is not constrained by their label.

EXERCISE

Think of a label you give your child and see if you can come up with a sentence that describes the behaviour instead.

Alistair's Story

Alistair had a diagnosis of Attention Deficit Hyperactivity Disorder (ADHD). He needed help with planning his time. When his parents gave him a series of commands such as go upstairs, brush your teeth, wash your face, and get dressed, he would forget the third instruction by the time he'd brushed his teeth. His parents found his behaviour exhausting. They felt close to thinking he was being purposely disobedient. Alistair also had very low self-esteem. When I asked him what he was good at or what made him special, he couldn't think of a single thing.

During one of the family sessions, we spent time drawing a timeline to represent the different activities that Alistair had to do in the morning and evening. This greatly helped him to be able to organise himself. I then used strength cards in a session where he and his sister, brother and parents had to choose a card which depicted a strength to describe each other, such as kind, brave or enthusiastic. This session enabled Alistair to see that he did have strengths and to express his positive feelings towards the rest of his family. He started to see that he was unique and special. Alistair's parents were delighted by how he was now starting to manage his ADHD and become more confident.

If a child has a disability or they were very vulnerable as a baby, the parents can feel very protective of them, but this can then give rise to a secondary handicap. The child is being protected from the world and not allowed to experience success and failure, or how they can have an effect on their world. In these instances, the initial label (such as fragile, vulnerable or helpless) can cause more problems in the future.

EXERCISE

Take a moment to think back to when you were a child or teenager. Did your parents ever use terms to describe you such as 'naughty', 'bad', 'selfish', 'inconsiderate' or other negative labels? How did it feel to be labelled critically by your parents or by any other adult in your early life? What does it feels like now to be labelled critically by another adult, or even by your children?

Labelling: Key points

★ Labelling can create a self-fulfilling prophecy.
★ Labelling can develop into roles in children which are unhelpful, especially in a group of brothers and sisters.
★ Describing behaviour is much more helpful than labelling the child, as it separates the child from the behaviour.

Chapter 7

Helping Children to Solve Problems

This chapter gives children the tools to help them sort out their own problems. When children are empowered to do this, it increases their self-esteem as they know they have the skills to make good decisions.

When children are upset, it is important to listen to them and acknowledge their feelings. It is also important to try to teach them how to solve their own problems. One technique for doing this is to help the child think of a whole list of possible solutions, look at each one of them and think, 'What would be the consequences?'

When the child is thinking about the consequences of each suggestion it is important to encourage them to think about everyone's feelings too, to help them develop empathy. The child also learns that there can be many solutions to a problem. Once you've chosen a solution together and put it into practice, you can talk about how successful it was. This teaches children the importance of following things through and also of learning from either the positive or negative outcomes of their solution.

When I work with children I draw a spider diagram and let the child choose how many legs they want to put around the spider's tummy; then we all think of that number of solutions. I encourage the child to be as creative as possible because a good idea can sometimes come out of what at first may have seemed completely absurd. Then we go through each solution in depth to see if they would work . We discard the ones that seem impractical or difficult. Then we are left with a couple that could work which the child can then put into practice.

Ryan and Scott's Story

Ryan and his father Scott came to see me because he was not doing his homework or achieving at school. He was angry at his father for separating from his mother, and part of the reason for his failure to do his school work was to upset his father and keep him involved.

Scott was exasperated with Ryan, but when we did the problem-solving exercise they were both able to generate some new solutions. Ryan found maths difficult and so said he could try to ask his Dad to help with his homework. He liked to go skate-boarding straight after school, so Scott suggested going home first and doing homework before going skateboarding. Ryan said he was always hungry when he got home from school and couldn't think, so they decided that if he had some toast this might help. Ryan told his father that he was stupid anyway, so doing homework wouldn't make any difference. They decided to do an experiment to see what marks he got when he did his homework to see if this was true. From this exercise, Scott and Ryan discovered they were able to work together to come up with solutions, such as Ryan phoning his father if he got stuck with homework.

Molly and Katerina's Story

Molly and Katerina came to see me because Molly was having problems at school with her group of friends. We used the spider diagram to think up solutions. One advantage of this approach is that because you're working together with your child, you can put forward suggestions rather than telling them what to do. Katerina spoke about the importance of sometimes going along with what the group wanted to do, of not always needing to have your own way, about listening, and having empathy.

Molly suggested forming another friendship group, and ignoring one of the girls who was teasing her. She also came up with the idea of developing a new game that all the girls could play together. Katerina said that she could invite some of the girls home for a play-date.

The Nowak Family's Story

The Nowak family came to see me because they were arguing and screaming at each other and the four sons never did what they were told.

When the whole family sat down to discuss what they could do to stop all the arguments they came up with a lot of solutions, which to their parents' surprise included having a family night in every week and playing a board game or watching a film. They also suggested ways the boys could respect each other's space even though they shared a bedroom.

Try practising this problem-solving activity if your child comes to you with a problem that they want help with, or if you think you could support them with a new approach to a problem.

Helping Children Solve Problems: Key Points

★   Helping children solve their own problems can empower them in the future.

★   Creating a spider diagram with the problem in the middle and solutions on each leg can help children become creative problem-solvers.

★   Parents can offer solutions as a way of giving advice which doesn't leave the child feeling defensive.

★   Helping children go through the consequences of each suggestion improves their problem-solving abilities and empathy for others.

★   Children learn to understand that there can be lots of solutions to one problem.

Chapter 8

The Meaning of Children's Behaviour

It is useful to understand that all behaviour has a meaning that can be interpreted by trying to understand the need that underlies the behaviour. This is crucial in trying to work out how to respond to that behaviour.

No behaviour happens in a vacuum. Behaviour – even when it appears strange – is always about meeting a need. Everything we do is driven by these needs, which are in large part common to both adults and children. There are three crucial groups of emotional and psychological need.

The first concerns acceptance from others, including the need for attention (even negative attention is better than no attention), for belonging, for feeling accepted and loved.

Another kind of need is for freedom – for example, the need to have a sense of independence, and to be free to explore and learn.

Finally, there is a need for rules and fairness, a need for security, and for clear and upheld boundaries.

The need expressed by a child's behaviour is the most important issue for parents to work out, because then they may not feel so angry or perplexed. They can then address the need directly rather than being angered by the behaviour. Here are a few common examples to illustrate these behaviours.

Attention – A child may start shouting when you're on the phone because they want your attention.

Belonging – A child who doesn't want to go upstairs to bed and leave his parents watching television together.

Independence – A child who may want to wear their own, inappropriate clothes for school.

Security – A child may not want to leave their mother's side when they go out to a social event.

Explore and learn – A child who pours flour on the floor and plays at making patterns.

Useful – A child may start taking all the clothes out of the washing machine on to the floor.

Boundaries – A child who picks up a sweet at the shop and then looks at his father to see the reaction.

As a parent you may get it wrong sometimes and not be able to sort out what the need is behind the behaviour, but it is a useful framework to have. Parenting can become much happier if we're curious about the needs behind our children's behaviour. Sometimes parents can attribute very adult-like emotions and thoughts to young children and think that they're being manipulative on purpose. However, children under six are not able to consciously manipulate their parents, as they don't have the intellectual ability to put themselves in their parents' shoes.

Joyce's Story

I was seeing Joyce and her three children for family therapy and the six year-old son started to become very upset. He was writing down all the household rules he thought were important, but couldn't spell all the words so he crunched the paper up and started to have a tantrum. Joyce tried to control his behaviour by telling him to calm down and behave. I interjected and said, 'It's so frustrating when you really want to get the words right and look neat and then it all gets spoilt by a spelling mistake'. The son calmed down immediately – the meaning of his behaviour was frustration at a spelling mistake and the need was to write perfectly.

Amanda's Story

Amanda was a perfectionist. Her writing and pictures could not contain any mistakes – in this way she was similar to her mother. During our sessions we developed a 'mistakes book' – every time anyone made a mistake it was written in the book and celebrated. This helped to achieve more balance in Amanda's behaviour. She no longer had a tantrum if she made a little mistake, but asked her mother to put it in the special book.

Stephen, Agnes, and Pete's Story

Stephen was refusing to go to school. His parents were not getting on and there were many arguments at home.

Stephen's parents, Agnes and Pete, came to see me because he'd already missed two terms of school. As I listened to Agnes and Pete, I wondered whether Stephen's behaviour of not going to school may have been directly caused by his parents' relationship. He had found a fool-proof method to get his parents to talk to each other, even if it was only about him, and even to come to therapy. When we then had some sessions of couple work and then family therapy, Stephen started to go back to school in a phased manner. Stephen also suffered from anxiety, but he was able to learn ways of coping with this during the family therapy sessions from his father, who also had learned methods to cope with the same condition.

Remember something that you used to do that your parents or carers didn't like. What do you think you were trying to achieve by behaving in that way? What was it about the behaviour that led your parent or carer to become upset about it? Now think about something that your child does that upsets you, and what your child is trying to achieve through that behaviour.

When thinking about a child's behaviour you sometimes need to be a detective to work out the underlying reasons. In complex situations involving trauma, loss, adoption and so on, the reason may be very deep-rooted in the unconscious, and the parent, carer or therapist needs to be very skilled to see what is being played out in the troubling situations.

In cases of adoption or fostering, the child may draw out from the foster-carers or adoptive parents the same behaviour he experienced when he was being traumatized in his original family. This can be very confusing for the carers, who can't understand what they've done to cause it. For example, the child may unconsciously provoke anger from the adoptive father to see if he'll be hit, as he once was himself as a small child. This means that the carer has to be very vigilant not to respond reactively, without thinking of the context of the behaviour and the child's perspective. Unlocking past experiences can be the key to understanding a child's behaviour.

David's Story

David was terrified of going back to playing rugby. He was 11 years old and had three recent injuries, one having been very serious in which he broke an arm falling off play equipment. He'd twisted his ankle and had also banged his head while playing on the trampoline.

David had been a very good rugby player. It had been one of his passions, but now whenever he went even close to the rugby pitch he started to get very nervous and would refuse to get out of the car when he arrived. He told his parents that he now hated the game. His parents were very concerned and couldn't understand his behaviour. In our sessions, I explained to David's parents that sometimes, memories got buried in the child's brain and had to be brought up to consciousness so they could be examined, accepted and understood by the conscious mind – otherwise they can induce fear, avoidance and upset. The memory could stop the child doing something that they would normally have liked to do.

David's parents were able to speak about how traumatic David's experience of breaking his arm had been. In my sessions with David, he spoke about the accident when he broke his arm in great detail. We also used creative materials (paints and clay) to draw and model his different experiences in the hospital, so the experience was brought back up to his consciousness. When we got to the difficult part when his arm was being realigned, he often didn't want to speak of that, so we jumped that bit and went to the happy ending when his arm felt better and he was not in pain.

Soon afterwards he was able to talk about having his arm realigned as well. After eight weeks, the buried memory of how he'd broken his arm and had it treated had come to the surface. It was integrated as a normal memory so that he no longer felt so frightened of hurting himself, and he was able to return to playing rugby.

Grief can cause much behaviour that seems strange and uncharacteristic. Understanding grief and the stages in bereavement can help to some extent in families that have been affected by death.

Sophie's Story

Sophie had experienced the death of her twin in traumatic circumstances four years previously when she was 13. She was now in the final year of her A-levels and, after having had a spotless career at school, she was drinking and taking drugs, and her attendance at school had plummeted. She had insisted that her younger brother and sister, as well as her parents, came with her to family therapy. Her parents Diane and Kevin were happy to attend as they were so worried about her.

During the sessions it turned out that no one in the family had been able to speak about the death. On the surface everything had gone on as normal, but they'd not been able to grieve together. Sophie wanted to talk about her twin and make sure her siblings did as well, so they wouldn't experience the pain of having no outlet for their grief. The parents were also able to speak about their child who'd died and bring in all her belongings such as school books, clothes and toys. Sophie's acting-out behaviour had been to bring her family to therapy so that they could grieve for their sister and child together.

The Meaning of Behaviour: Key Points

★   No behaviour happens in a vacuum; it always has a meaning.

★   There is always a need behind the behaviour, however obscure it might be.

★   The commonest needs children have are for attention, belonging, security, to be able to explore and learn, to be independent, to have boundaries and to feel useful.

Chapter 9

Discipline Strategies

This chapter gives an overview of discipline methods that are effective and respectful of the child. Parents often come to a parenting group because they want to learn discipline strategies to help them stop their child misbehaving. However, it is often the case that when parents have started implementing the more positive behaviours described in the earlier chapters, such as child-led play or descriptive praise, the misbehaviour has already ceased.

There is a common misconception that discipline means to punish a child. But to discipline means to educate, and is of enormous importance in helping children know right from wrong – to become adults with an intrinsic sense of how to behave in society towards other people.

When children are very young, discipline is often exerted through external controls, such as the parent telling their child to be kind to another, to look after their belongings, or to go to bed when asked. It then becomes internalized, and the child doesn't need to be told what to do but behaves this way naturally. However, discipline can sometimes be a difficult issue because of our own family scripts from past generations about discipline, power and control.

Sometimes we lack conviction in what we say. The child then picks that up and doesn't follow our instruction. Sometimes we may think that how we were parented was too harsh, so we want to do it completely differently: our discipline may become very lax, with the result that we're not respected by our children. If we are having a bad day and feeling exhausted, the last thing we want to do is enforce the house rules. The easiest thing in the short term is to give in and not have a fight. However, this merely stores up problems for the future.

The importance of discipline is that it helps a child feel secure, able to explore and learn, but within clear boundaries. It is important because it helps a child become socialized so that they will fit into society and be able to function. A child who has not learned that it's unkind and unacceptable to hit other children when they want their toy is unlikely to have many friends. Discipline helps a child make friends and fit into their social world. Discipline is also important for physical safety, so that children understand not to go where a barrier says 'No entry', or to stop when their mother calls out 'Stop' near a busy road. It also helps children realise that all their actions have consequences: for example, if they behave badly on a shopping trip they might not be able to go the following week. External discipline can then become internalized as the child grows emotionally and matures.

Carol and Kevin's Story

Carol was a young mother with an energetic six year-old son who was 'into everything'. He wouldn't do what he was told, however, and she was furious with him a lot of the time as she felt belittled by his constant refusal to do what he was told. Carol had the very difficult task of bringing up her son on her own as his father had died. She also had a very complex relationship with discipline because her own parents had been very strict, not hesitating to beat her with a belt. She was desperate not to be like her own parents, so felt unable to discipline him at all. She would then suddenly lose her temper when she had been pushed too hard, screaming and yelling at her son.

Carol and I worked together for six sessions on developing a set of household rules and what strategies she could use to enforce them. By the end of the sessions she felt much stronger in being able to use discipline. Kevin was much happier, feeling secure with his mother, and they also spent more time doing positive activities together.

For Very Young Children

Discipline for very little children is complicated because before they're about 2 years of age, they have no concept of right and wrong but just want what they want. Most of the techniques in this chapter are aimed at children over two-and-a-half. A child under three can become very angry and upset if they don't get their own way. This is part of their development of the understanding that they can affect their environment. Sometimes distraction can be the answer in these circumstances. The child is not wilfully misbehaving. They have no concept of the parent as a separate mind with a different agenda. The toddler wants what it wants now! Thus, being creative as a parent and having lots of interesting items in your pocket such as key rings, shiny pieces of paper, or a toy that makes a noise can all be used to stop a major meltdown about not getting another biscuit.

Household Rules

Having household rules makes life much easier for children as they know what's expected and everything is clear. Children can get very confused if rules are only implicit and they're not sure what the boundaries are. It is much easier to be consistent if the household rules are explicit. All families will have different household rules, as this is the way parents pass on some of their values to the next generation.

For example the rules could be: no violence, no swearing, take your shoes off at the front door, come home at an agreed time, no TV before school, dirty clothes go into the laundry basket, sweets only on Friday. This chapter looks at some methods to ensure these rules are respected.

Yasmin's Story

I was working with a family in which the child seemed to take delight in being cruel to her mother, Yasmin. The child didn't want to sit beside her, eat her food or be tucked up in bed by her. She pinched and hurt her. When we discussed setting rules, Yasmin was terrified at the prospect. Their daughter had cried for five hours when she was not allowed to play with her iPad. Yasmin was at breaking-point and wanted to leave home because she was feeling so upset by her daughter. We worked through many sessions together, helping Yasmin to set boundaries and household rules using the skills covered in this chapter, and also to build up the attachment using praise and child-led play. After eight weeks Yasmin had a much better relationship with her daughter.

Routines

Routines are similar to household rules in that the child knows what's expected, making life much more predictable and less stressful. Having a set routine – such as, brush teeth, wash face, put on clothes, come downstairs, have breakfast, go to school – can make the morning much easier to manage. Some children, who are more emotionally impulsive, find life much easier with routines. If you have a large family, it also makes managing the children and helping them all feel secure much more straightforward.

EXERCISE

With your partner and the children, write down what you'd like the household rules to be in your family.

Giving Limited Choice

This is a way of giving a child respect and autonomy while retaining their co-operation, which is very effective with younger children. For example, you can say, 'Would you like a small spoon of yogurt or a big one? ... 'Do you want to lay the table or put the toys in the box?' ... 'Would you like to help play gently with George or go to your room?'

Active Ignoring

This is one of the most straightforward discipline methods. Positive behaviour is rewarded and negative behaviour is not. For example, when a child is behaving badly at the table you don't reinforce the behaviour by telling your child off, but ignore it and give your attention to the other child who is behaving well. Very soon, the misbehaving child will want some of your attention and so start behaving well again.

Active ignoring means looking away from your child and not offering any reaction to their behaviour. It is very useful for small misdemeanours like whinging, swearing (especially in a small child who doesn't know what they're saying but just knows it gets a great reaction), fake temper-tantrums, minor squabbles between brothers and sisters, and protests when told 'no'.

Benedicte and Anja's Story

Benedicte was very unhappy that her 8 year-old daughter, Anja, regularly played up at dinner time. She was committed to having a family meal together around the table every evening, as she felt that this meant that they were being a proper family. However, the stress this caused her was making her question this commitment. She felt like giving up and just letting the kids eat in front to the TV.

When Benedicte and her partner came to see me, we analysed what was happening when Anja got up from the dinner table and started to make a commotion with her younger brother. This meant she got a lot of attention from her father, who would be telling her to behave and not spoil the meal for everyone else. She would then get more attention when she left the table, as her mother came after her, trying to make her come back and not wreck the evening. It would often end up with Anja being sent to bed, with everyone feeling stressed and unhappy.

On trying active ignoring as a technique, Benedicte and Mannus were thrilled to see how quickly their daughter came back to the table when they ignored her and focused attention on their son. They did not make a big issue of it when their daughter returned to the table, but just included her in their conversation. They were soon all able to enjoy eating together in the evening.

Giving Commands

How parents give commands is the key to getting children to take them seriously. It's the way you say something that conveys the message much more convincingly than the actual words. Rather than yelling, 'Put the TV off!', bend down to be face-to-face with your child and say 'Put the TV off now', in a firm voice while making eye contact. This is a far more powerful way of showing the child you really mean it. A common mistake would be to say, 'Would you like to put the TV off now, please?' – to which the child can easily just say 'No', creating an immediate conflict. Here are some points to bear in mind when giving a command:

• **Think first about whether you're prepared to make sure it's carried out. Remember, the difference between a command and a request is that you're not prepared to give in.**

• **Commands work best when you have the child's attention before telling them what you want, so make sure you have eye contact and they know that you're talking to them.**

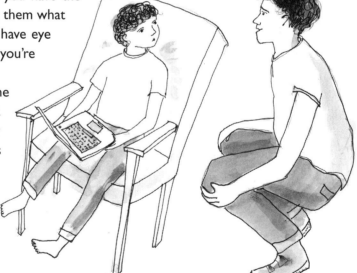

• **Sometimes children need time to comply. Children will test out their parents to see if they really have to do a task so it's best not to be impatient.**

• **It's best to avoid commands that are vague, emotional, questioning or pleading.**

Angela's Story

Angela was exhausted. She felt that her children never listened to her and she spent all her time yelling at them to do the smallest task. After coming for some sessions of support she started to feel a little stronger in herself and to build up her self-esteem. She decided to limit commands to things she felt really strongly about. She was then able to give commands in a voice consistent with her body language. She was amazed when her children started to do what she commanded.

Consequences

When we use consequences it's very important that:

- **they are relevant and age-appropriate**
- **you're able and willing to carry them through**
- **you've told the child beforehand what the consequence will be, thus giving them the choice over their actions**
- **if the child is young, that the consequences are immediate**

Consequences can be natural (for example, if a child breaks a toy, the toy is no longer useable) or logical (if a child plays with a ball in the living room, it gets taken away). Making statements can be a useful way of using consequences to avoid the child losing face because they make the decision – for example, 'Either we can tidy up the room and go to the park or we can stay at home ... You can either stop throwing the ball inside and go outside or have no ball at all to play with.'

Jayden's Story

Mr and Mrs Mackintosh came to see me because they were concerned about their 12 year-old son Jayden's obsession with gaming on the computer.

If they didn't intervene he would happily spend from 4.30 p.m. to 11 p.m. on the computer every school day, and all day at the weekend.

He would go into a fury when his parents asked him to come off the computer and was refusing to go out to see his friends or go on family outings.

His language towards his parents at these times when they did try to enforce boundaries was horrendous.

In working with the Mackintoshes I first had to emphasize the damage that continual gaming could do for Jayden and the impact it was having on his school work and social skills. With both parents totally committed to doing the best for Jayden, they instigated a plan to help him become less addicted to the computer games.

They had a family meeting, told Jayden their concerns about his continual gaming and said they were going to set limits on it. They then negotiated together when he could use the computer. They agreed together that 1.5 hours on school days from 7 to 8.30 p.m. was acceptable but only after he had completed his homework. They also planned to all eat together at 6.30 p.m.

At weekends they agreed that he had to go out with them if there were family activities such as going on a dog walk, but that he could play on the computer from 2 to 4 p.m. and then 7 till 9 if they were not out.

A consequence for breaking the rules was that he would have no screen time at all for the following day .

Mr Mackintosh manipulated the router so that Jayden could only access the Internet at these times.

It was a struggle for Jayden's parents to keep to these boundaries as Jayden fought hard against them and tried to manipulate his mother to give in, which would then lead to conflict between the parents. They also had to slightly change their life styles to include having more time together as a family and to stop being completely work orientated. There were many instances when Jayden had no screen time all weekend because he did not keep to the rules. His behaviour got worse before he realised he had to accept the boundaries, and then slowly he started to comply as he realised his parents were serious. However, Jayden did slowly start to enjoy family time and his parents started spending many more fun times with him.

Consequences must be non-punitive – for example, don't bite the child if they bite. The child will feel resentful towards the parent and be less likely to change their behaviour. One mother told her son that she would take him to school in his pyjamas if he didn't get up, but was too mortified to carry it out. This led to the child feeling even more powerful. In such an instance, a logical consequence like not having the iPad for a day is much more manageable.

Another consequence which can be useful for some children is to ask them to make up for the wrong that they've done. This can sometimes be more effective than taking an hour of their screen time – for example, drawing a picture for mum to say sorry for being rude, or helping to clean the car if they'd been fighting in the car.

Tom's Story

Tom was on his phone all the time. His parents were worried he was not getting enough sleep or time away from social media. They told Tom that if he was on his smartphone after 10 p.m., the phone would be taken away and kept in his parents' bedroom until the morning. This logical consequence enabled Tom to get a good night's sleep, and his parents did not need to worry about him being tired in the morning.

A word of caution: some children – this may include children who have been traumatized, have Attention Deficit Hyperactivity Disorder, Autistic Spectrum Disorder or sensory processing problems – find it hard to use any rational thinking when they are distressed. Negative consequences may make little sense when they're upset because at the point of distress they find it hard to think ahead or to see the sequence of events that has led to the reprimand. These children often need frequent small rewards to help develop acceptable behaviour because they have a reduced capacity to adapt their behaviour themselves.

Externalizing

Externalizing is a technique used in family therapy. It has been very successful at changing behaviour because it doesn't blame the child and enables everyone to think about the problem from one step removed. Externalizing is when the problematic behaviour is thought about as separate from the child. It can be discussed objectively without blaming. For example, if a child is stealing, by thinking with the child about the problem (stealing) and calling it a name like 'Mr Wants-It-Now', they can discuss when 'Mr Wants-It-Now' is very strong and when he is weak. They can then put into practice all the ideas that they come up with for when 'Mr Wants-It-Now' is very weak. This could be when the child is busy, when he feels loved or when he has his favourite toy in his pocket. They could also think with their child about other feelings that come up together with 'Mr Wants-It-Now', such as jealousy or feeling unimportant.

Leo's Story

Leo's parents brought him to see me, as they were concerned about his temper-tantrums and aggressive behaviour. During the session I asked Leo to draw the anger in him which was causing the temper-tantrums. He drew a graphic picture of a monster with flames coming out of his mouth. He then decided to call him 'Terence the Terrible Temper Tantrum'. We were then able to consider with his parents what made Terence stronger or weaker. In this way, Leo and his parents were able to beat Terence the Terrible Temper Tantrum because they knew what made him weaker. Leo was able to tell his parents that Terence became weaker when he went out on a cycle ride or a walk with his dad, and when he was not being teased by his brother and sister. From the parents first coming to me with worries that Leo had 'pathological demand avoidance', they were able to see that together they could all tackle Terence. Within four weeks Leo's behaviour had improved dramatically.

Ada, Idowu and Barack's Story

Ada and Idowu came to see me about their 7 year-old son Barack who had a diagnosis of ADHD with Autism Spectrum Disorder traits. Barack was refusing to eat solid food since a painful visit to the dentist. He would scream and hit his parents if they tried to make him eat just one mouthful of solid food.

I used the technique of externalizing and I worked with Barack and his parents to think of a name we could call the worry that was leading him to refuse solid food. Barack decided to call the worry 'Mr Smelly'. Barack and his parents all drew a picture of Mr Smelly. We all thought together how to beat Mr Smelly so that Barack could eat solid food again. Barack got excited thinking of ways to sneak food past Mr Smelly and his parents also thought of some good ideas. These ideas involved running, eating in the garden, eating with your eyes shut. I saw the family again after two weeks and Barack had beaten Mr Smelly – he was now able to eat solid food, and his parents were delighted with how strong Barack had been in his fight against Mr Smelly.

Rewards

Star charts, stickers, point systems, marbles in a jar and positive messages are all ways of reinforcing positive behaviour. They can be successful in encouraging the behaviour you want, but do entail the parent staying motivated and maintaining the reward system.

Sometimes parents are worried about giving rewards because they feel it is like bribery. However, it is only bribery if you give it beforehand – such as giving a child a computer game if they promise to revise for their exams. This is often unsuccessful. The statement 'When you … then …' is a useful template for giving a reward, e.g. 'When you finish doing your homework you can watch 30 minutes of television'. The statement 'If you ….. then…' is much more tentative, and so you are much less likely to be successful.

Star Charts

The key points in setting up a star chart system are:

- They are good for children aged 3–8.
- They need to work on one very specific behaviour that you want to change.
- Children need to be able to succeed with them, and so make the steps very small – for example, getting into bed at 7 p.m. for two nights gets a reward.
- Stars should never be taken away.
- Phrase behaviours positively – for example, 'playing gently together for 30 minutes', not 'no fighting for 30 minutes'.
- Let the child choose what is rewarding for them, within limits.
- It helps if the child designs the start chart with help from a parent.
- The parent must keep control of the star chart.

Star charts are very effective for quickly changing problem behaviour. Their success is due to the fact that they motivate the child to get the reward, and success further motivates the child. The new behaviour soon becomes a habit.

Example Star Charts
1. Staying in bed all night

	Monday	Tuesday	Wednesday	Thursday	Friday	Saturday	Sunday
Week 1							
Week 2							

2. Getting dressed before 8 a.m.

Monday	Tuesday	Wednesday	Thursday	Friday	Saturday	Sunday

Move the arrow along the steps until it reaches Superman.

3. Putting toys away once you have finished playing with them

Colour in the parts of the dog.

Danielle and Conner's Story

Danielle came to a parenting group because her son with autism, Connor, was hard to manage. She found it especially hard to get him dressed and out of the house for school. Conner was obsessed by vacuum cleaners, and Danielle had the brilliant idea of doing a picture of the outline of the vacuum cleaner at home and dividing it into five sections. When Conner got dressed and into the car he was able to colour in one section of the vacuum cleaner. This proved successful at helping Conner get ready in the mornings.

Yanna's Story

Yanna's three year-old daughter hated putting her coat on in the morning when it was cold outside. Yanna created a picture of a coat with dots on it that needed to be filled in. When her daughter put the coat on she was able to fill in a dot. After two days she no longer complained about putting her coat on.

Kumari's Story

Kumari was fed up because her four and six year-old sons fought together all the time after school. She created a star chart where they would both get a star if they played well together from 4.30 till 5. The boys were able to do this and the behaviour spread to other times as well, so they spent much less time fighting.

Kirsty and Tyrone's Story

Kirsty was on a parenting course and explained she was at her wits end with her six year-old son Tyrone, who was being threatened with expulsion because of his violent behaviour. The school instigated a reward chart system every week for her child. The chart was filled with stamps if he had a good day and there were no incidents of violence. At the end of each week the reward chart was put in a folder. After three weeks Tyrone had three reward charts covered in stamps saying, 'Well done ... Good behaviour ... Top man', and so on. He was thrilled and much happier at school. Kirsty was also proud of his accomplishment in managing his anger. Tyrone was also beginning to make more friends at school.

EXERCISE

With your child create a star chart to change a behaviour that is causing a problem.

Stickers

Stickers can also be very motivating for younger children. They can be put on the child's shirt or on their hand. In my own work I create stickers on adhesive address labels, depending on the issue a child may have. For example, positive statements such as 'Good listening..., Good sitting', and so on. Other stickers that I create are pictures of beds, if the issues are going to bed, or pictures of clothes, if the issue is putting clothes on.

Jim and Shaun's Story

Jim came to see me about his four year-old child son Shaun, who wouldn't go to bed. I made some stickers with a picture of a bed on them. Shaun was thrilled to get these stickers if he went to bed with no fuss, and the bedtime problem disappeared.

Home Point Systems

Once children are over eight years of age, a star chart may seem childish and so a home points system can be helpful. Add an extra zero to the points so that they seem greater and more motivating and exciting for the child. It does need a lot more commitment and management from the parent, though, as you have to actually tally up all the points every night or the system will not work.

Do more of these	Points each is worth	Points that you've earned						
		Mon	Tues	Wed	Thurs	Fri	Sat	Sun
Out of bed by 7 a.m.	100	—						
Unload the dishwasher	300	300						
Shower every morning	100	100						

TOTAL POINTS   **400**

Rewards	Points each cost	Points that you've spent						
		Mon	Tues	Wed	Thurs	Fri	Sat	Sun
Staying up for 'Match of the Day'	200	—						
Extra hour on computer game	200	200						
Choosing favourite meal	180	—						

TOTAL POINTS   **200**

Home point systems are very effective for children over eight and for pre-adolescents. For young people with Attention Deficit Hyperactivity Disorder (ADHD) it can be extremely effective, as it is concrete and seen as a challenge.

Marbles in a Jar

If you are working with a group of brothers and sisters, it may be best to use a rewards system for all of them. If all the children play well together in the evening, they can get a marble in the jar. When the jar is full, all the children can have a treat – for example, going to the swimming pool, playing a family game together, or whatever they find rewarding. The beauty of the marble jar is that all the children support each other to behave well, so that they can all get the treat at the end. Some parents have adapted the marble-in-the jar strategy to sweets in the jar, then the sweets get divided out to share at the weekend.

Liam, Oscar and Poppy's Story

Liam, Oscar and Poppy fought all the time. They were very close in age, with only four years separating them, and all were competing for their parent's attention. There were often fights over the smallest of issues, such as who was first in the car, who sat next to mummy, or who could hold mummy's hand.

With other strategies in place, such as all the children having some child-led play, the marble jar proved effective. If the children played well together from after school till bedtime, they would get a marble in the jar. They were soon much happier playing together and got out of the habit of always fighting.

Rewards – Further Thoughts

It can be motivating to offer children rewards such as choosing what to eat for dinner or staying up to watch a special programme. An extension of this is a 'magic bag' that has small presents wrapped up in it (from a pound shop or equivalent). If you think the children have been especially well-behaved, they could have a surprise present from the magic bag. This is very reinforcing because it is unexpected. Unexpected rewards or consequences have the additional benefit that the child does not feel that he has been controlled in any way. The good behaviour comes from their own intrinsic motivation.

Be careful not to link doing family chores with your child's pocket money. This can lead to children saying they will not help unless they get paid for it, and asking for more money to complete other jobs. Children often want to do chores to demonstrate that they have an important role in keeping the family functioning well.

Rewards can also be cuddles, hugs or kisses. Some parents find it difficult being visibly physically demonstrative, but touch is a powerful medium and can convey much more than words. Just one hug can be enormously rewarding as it gives a feeling of being held and loved.

Positive Messages

In some schools, children who are finding it difficult to conform to the school rules are given messages after each lesson on a slip of paper with a star on it, describing what they did well. These positive messages get put into their folder so at the end of the week they open up a great collection of positive statements. This can have a very constructive effect on their school behaviour.

Challenging

If the reward-based discipline methods are used exclusively, they can lead to a parent feeling that they always have to give the child something in exchange for good behaviour. It's good to also use a different, direct method of discipline, such as the Four-part Statement described in Chapter 2.

Alesha's Story

Alesha, a lone parent, was telling the parenting group how frustrated she was with her three children because they left their dirty plates and mugs in their bedrooms. With the support of the group she wrote down the Four-part I Message she wanted to tell her children: 'I feel frustrated when I see dirty plates and mugs in your bedrooms because they belong in the kitchen. How can you help me with this problem?'

The children thought for a while and then said they would take their dirty plates and mugs and put them in the dishwasher.

The other parents in the group helped Alesha see that adding too many reasons – such as, we'll get mice in the flat, it looks disgusting, I'm exhausted, you're so selfish – would be counterproductive. If we want to change behaviour, our communication should be clean – clear and not inflammatory. It's also important to keep the message short, or the point of the challenge gets lost in too many words.

If a child is very upset, challenging may not work – remember that everyone needs their emotional thermometer to be mid-way, not boiling, to be able to hear and respond rationally. Also, if you're not that upset by a behaviour but feel you ought to be 'because of what other people will think', then the challenge may not come across as sincere and will not be effective.

Saying 'No' – Setting Limits and Being Firm and Gentle

Saying 'no' could be for practical reasons – for example, 'No, you can't go and stay with your friend after school as I have to go out this evening and need you home'. It could be for security reasons in situations of risk – for example, 'No, you can't go to the park by yourself'. There are times when your needs will take priority over those of your child, and you'll insist on something being done or not done. This is fine and healthy, and no reason to feel guilty! In fact, you are reinforcing for your child a very important point that parents are in charge, which stops the child feeling too powerful and then scared of their power.

When you put aside being democratic and lay down the law, either saying 'no' to a request or insisting something is done, it's important to:

- **be sure you've thought out your reasons**
- **use non-blaming language**
- **remain calm and detached**
- **be clear that it's a non-negotiable situation**

To use this calm 'soft no' effectively we have to feel quiet and confident on the inside, so that we can express it in such a real way that our child will totally accept it.

EXERCISE

If you find saying 'no' difficult, practise with a friend. Ask them to role-play your child wanting to have some biscuits before dinner, or whatever the issue is you're dealing with. Ask your friend to be as persuasive as possible. Then practise saying 'no', giving one explanation, and then just repeating 'no' and letting your voice get quieter and quieter. Try staying soft on the inside as you clearly state 'No', being consistent in your expressions and voice. This will help when you actually have to say it to your child.

Family Meetings

Meetings are a good way for family members to communicate with each other. They can stop small issues growing into enormous ones because they've not been talked about and sorted out. They're useful for planning family outings and holidays, agreeing household rules, and as a place to bring up and solve problems.

Family meetings are especially helpful for step-families when there can be lots of issues to sort out, such as different ways of doing things, feeling things are not fair, arguments between children, or when individuals feel that their needs are not being met.

It is important that everyone gets an opportunity to talk. If everyone talks at once, try the 'hat rule' – pass around a hat, then whoever's holding the hat gets to speak without being interrupted. Tell the family a few days beforehand that you want to have a family meeting. Ask them to think about any issues they want to bring up, so that they can bring them to the meeting.

Choose a good time for the family meeting. Sitting at a table can help. Before a meal can be a good time because then everyone has the meal to look forward to. It is important to ask all the family members to attend. Explain that the purpose of the meeting is to help the home run smoothly. Make sure to switch the TV off and ask people to put mobile phones and other devices aside, so that the meeting gets everyone's full attention.

EXERCISE

Try holding a family meeting.

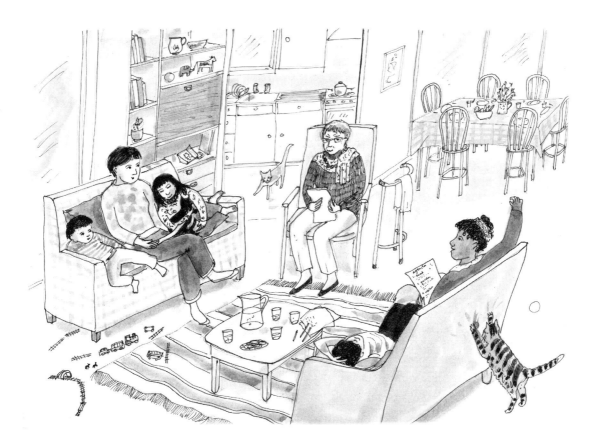

While my colleague and I were running an 'Understanding teenagers' course, we asked participants about their memories of family meetings. Two of the group said that in their family-of-origin, their parents had called a family meeting only to tell them that they were getting divorced. They therefore had very negative memories of a family meeting.

Paulina, Carla and Richard's Story

Paulina came to see me because her daughter was destroying her relationship with her partner Richard, whom she wanted to marry. Carla, aged 13, was adamant that her mother's partner was horrible, uncaring and hated her. She said that she would go and live with her father permanently if they got married. Carla's sister, Stacey, was much more neutral and involved in her own life and friendships.

Paulina set up a family meeting with her partner and the two girls. The family meeting helped Richard understand that Carla needed to have one-to-one time with her mother without him. Carla was able to see that Richard had feelings, and that he did help by picking her up from school and her friend's house when she asked. Although Carla and Richard never became close, they were able to all live together.

Negotiation

Negotiation is especially useful for parents of teenagers, as you can't use the same discipline techniques with a teenager that you use with a five year-old child. There has to be more give and take. Here are some examples in a template I use with parents of teenagers when they're in conflict or disagreement.

- 'I'm concerned when you ... don't get out of bed on time.'
- 'I feel ... upset and worried that you'll be late for school.'
- 'I think maybe you feel ...' (Try to understand the issue from the teenager's point of view – for example, 'tired and stressed'.)
- 'And this is what I would like to happen ... you get up by 7.30.'
- Find out what they feel and what they'd like to happen too – for example, 'mum to stop nagging'.
- Discuss the options; agree a plan of action and then monitor it.

When negotiating with teenagers it's important to stick to the main issue, focusing on the behaviour not the person, and trying to understand the issue from the teenager's point of view. Say how you feel about the issue and what you'd like to happen, and find out how your teenager feels and what they would like to happen too. Finally, discuss the options and agree a plan of action. Throughout the negotiation it's also important to show faith and confidence in the teenager through your words, gesture and tone.

Julia and Mark's Story

I was working with a family of amicably divorced parents, Julia and Mark, who were supporting each other to parent as best they could. Julia was much stricter than Mark, and so the son was forcing the boundaries with his mother about going to bed and getting ready for school in the morning. We used the template in a discussion around how to help the mornings not be such a nightmare. They were all able to negotiate that the son would be ready by 7.50 a.m. for the lift to school or not have a lift, and Julia promised not to nag. Just having the template gave both the parents and the teenager a vehicle to express their thoughts and emotions in a non-confrontational way (even though it did get heated at times).

EXERCISE

If you have a teenager, try using the template in order to negotiate a mutually acceptable solution to a difference or issue you're having.

Time Out

Time Out is a discipline method in which the parent asserts their authority so the child learns to moderate their behaviour. The child has to sit on their own in a particular place for a short period of time. It's best to choose a neutral, empty place with no diversions where the child can't break anything – sitting on a step or in the hallway can be ideal. The child could also be at the other end of the room, but then it is important to make sure you do not make any eye contact and give any attention. Time Out only starts when the child is quiet.

It's best used with children between 3 and 8 years of age, and it gives a clear procedure for when the child's behaviour is either violent or totally defiant. It could be seen as a more educational alternative to smacking which is more powerful in changing behaviour. It is a great strategy to have when you feel on the brink of being violent or screaming because of their behaviour.

Time Out should be for one minute for each year of the child's age, lasting for a maximum of five minutes.

If the child has a history of being violent to others, you can talk to them when it's a calm and happy time, and explain that you want to help them learn to manage their violent outbursts. If they do ever hurt someone, therefore, they'll immediately be put in Time Out. The place for Time Out should be explained, and for how long (e.g. 4 minutes if they're aged four). For a child who is being defiant, the child is given a warning first, and has the opportunity to stop their behaviour before Time Out is implemented.

Time Out has had a mixed reception among parents, and is understood in many different ways. Some parents I've worked with feel that it's distressing and does not help the child's emotional development, while other parents feel it is of enormous value in reinforcing discipline. One mother used to put her four young sons in Time Out when they were fighting, each one on a separate step, and this helped to stop them fighting and to calm down, and so was extremely useful.

Time Out involves removing the child from the situation and having them sit on a stair or on the floor. If you're not at home you can use a piece of cloth with a circle on it that the child sits on – this has the merit of being transportable to different venues. The child is not asked to reflect on their behaviour, as the point of the exercise is for the child to appreciate that their parent is in charge so that they feel emotionally contained. By encouraging the child to think about what they've done and say 'sorry', you could re-stimulate the initial conflict. It's best to discuss the incident as soon as everyone is calmer so you can both work out what could have been done instead.

Sometimes it can be useful to think of the times when you're going to implement Time Out, such as if your child kicks their younger sister.

It is hard work, and you have to be determined to follow it through, and so having support is vital. When you tell your child to go to Time Out by the time I count to three, you can start to count out loud, 'that's one', then pause but staying calm and saying, 'that's two', and then 'that's three'. If they have not gone to Time Out you then need to take them there.

Exceptions for the Use of Time Out

Time Out should not be used with children who've been adopted or are fostered. It could trigger an abandonment response that they may have experienced in their original family. Time Out could then jeopardize the work you've done as an adoptive or foster parent to help the child feel secure with you. It is always important to think of the meaning of the behaviour, if your child had a tough start in life or is very anxious Time Out might not be the best strategy. Sometimes if you feel that a Time Out is necessary you may only need to do it for less than a minute, while the situation calms down.

A child who is on the autistic spectrum should not be put in Time Out because they may not understand the reason and feel very distressed, and it could make the situation much worse as they go into 'total melt down'.

Sometimes a child could hit out because they are very distressed. Then Time Out could be very distressing for them, in which case being close to the child by sitting with them will help contain the child but will also reinforce boundaries. This is sometimes known as Time In.

Parenting is an art, and every child and parent is unique. You will need to see what works for your family. The important concept to remember is that children feel safe and able to interact with the world if they have solid boundaries.

How to Use Time Out

- Give a clear command of what you expect from the child – for example, 'Stop screaming at your sister'
- If the command isn't obeyed, give a warning of time out
- If the command is then carried out, use descriptive praise
- If the command is not carried out, use Time Out
- A guideline for how long to leave the child in Time Out is one minute for each year of the child – three minutes for a three year old, up to a total of five minutes. The timing only starts when the child is quiet
- When Time Out is finished, tell the child it has finished and then continue as normal, but do reconnect

Wilhelm's Story

Bertha and Otto came to see me because they were worried about their youngest son Wilhelm who was fighting with his older brother continually and making family life unbearable.

Wilhelm seemed consumed with jealousy and would kick, pinch and punch his older brother, who had become very frightened of him. Bertha and Otto told me that they'd experienced great personal tragedy of the death of Wilhelm's younger sister to Sudden Infant Death Syndrome when Wilhelm was only two years old. Both Bertha and Otto had been overwhelmed by grief and so had not been able to give attention to their youngest son. Wilhelm was behaving in such an aggressive fashion because he'd learnt this was a way of getting attention from his parents when they had been unavailable. His jealousy of his brother was understandable in the context that neither of the children had received much attention, and so when his older brother did get to sit on his mother's lap or lie beside her in bed, he could not manage the strong feelings of anger that overwhelmed him.

However, this behaviour was totally unacceptable, and so with a mixed menu of other positive discipline strategies described earlier in the book, we also instigated Time Out.

When Wilhelm hurt his brother he immediately had to go to 'Time Out'. Time Out was situated on the first step of the stairs and his parents would take him there calmly after an aggressive incident and he had to sit there until he calmed down and then stay there for four minutes. For the first two times Wilhelm was angry when he was put in Time Out, but after these two times he went without a fuss. If a violent attack on his brother occurred when the family were out of the house, Bertha or Otto would put a cloth with a circle on it in a suitable quiet place on the ground, and then get Wilhelm to sit on it.

After only two weeks Wilhelm was no longer hitting his brother and they'd started to play together.

Francine's Story

Francine was upset by the birth of her baby brother. Francine's mother Miranda brought her to me because she was scared to leave a room if Francine was in it with the baby. She would try and scratch the babies face or 'play' with her in an aggressive, threatening way. Francine was three years old and Miranda had taken a career break from a rewarding and much-loved job to be with the children. Francine's husband worked very long hours and often left before the children woke up, and came home after they'd gone to bed. Miranda was exhausted, isolated and lonely and was not finding parenthood much fun. She knew she was short tempered with Francine and would often explode at her when she hurt the baby.

Together we planned a strategy for Miranda to get more of her own needs met by going to a keep-fit class, reconnecting with friends who had babies and having two hours at the weekend to go on a cycle ride with a good friend. Miranda also instigated the positive parenting strategies described earlier in the book. However, after two weeks Francine would still sometimes try to hurt the baby, and so Miranda instigated Time Out calmly and made Francine sit in the corridor of their flat for three minutes whenever she tried to hurt the baby.

This method proved very effective and Francine stopped hurting her baby brother. Miranda also started to enjoy parenting her two children and she became less isolated and gained confidence in her skills as a mother.

Reasons Not to Smack

Children have the capacity to make a parent so cross that they want to smack them hard. If you feel that way, however, it's very important to think about the following facts:

- As a parent you are a role model for your child. Aggression, threats or physical force all teach them that these are acceptable ways of dealing with conflict or disagreements.
- Smacking encourages children to learn how not to get caught.
- Children who are smacked can grow up angry and resentful and have low self-esteem. It also damages the relationship between you and your child.
- As a parent, if you smack your child too hard and then feel guilty and cuddle them, it can confuse your child. They may then think that violence is connected with love.

EXERCISE

Think back to a time in the past, from childhood or teens, when you would be told off by an adult for something they found unacceptable.
How were you challenged/told off by them?
How did you react and feel?
Did you want to change your behaviour as a result?

Parents often ask me whether Time Out is a soft option for children, and whether a good smack is what they really need. The problem with smacking is that the child then thinks that this has wiped the slate clean, that they don't need to think about what they have done. Time Out is much harder for children, because then they have to experience the uncomfortable feelings of responsibility and remorse.

Amma and Kofi's Story

Amma was on the parenting course because she had a three year-old, Kofi, who was completely out of control. He wouldn't listen to her. He ran away whenever she called him.

Throughout the course she had not spoken much, but had been listening intently to all the other parents, especially one who admitted to smacking her child when he would not eat. When the course finished, she described how she'd decided to stop smacking Kofi after the fourth session because she'd realised what a negative impact it was having. She was now going to make a commitment not to use smacking as a way of disciplining Kofi. She explained how she had previously kept a branch in every room of her flat to smack Kofi if he misbehaved. Amma had been brought up by very strict parents who used a lot of corporal punishment. She'd been beaten with a belt and a stick for any small misdemeanour, so this was the family script she was bringing to her parenting relationship with Kofi.

Because she was a recent immigrant to the United Kingdom, she felt especially strongly that Kofi must behave perfectly at all times. Her embarrassment and shame at his out-of-control behaviour had been fuelling her violent responses to him. This in turn had made his behaviour worse. After some follow-up sessions following the course, it was wonderful to see how her relationship with Kofi started to blossom, and they started to have fun together.

The parents on the course also met as a support group after it had ended. This helped Amma to feel connected with all the new friends she'd made, enabling her to keep on practising the new skills she'd learnt.

As a family therapist and parenting course facilitator, I know it can make an enormous difference if parents make a decision not to use physical punishment with their children. This decision then makes it much easier when you're feeling furious and want to lash out at your child. As parents, we can then focus on how to calm ourselves using stress-management techniques such as deep breathing, counting to ten, affirmations or visualizations (see Chapter 12). This leads to much better decision-making which is rational, and has a clear purpose to discipline, not punish.

Whose Problem Is It?

Problem ownership is a useful concept when thinking about your child's problem and how to manage it. This approach helps parents to prioritize their needs or their child's needs, and minimizes the risk of becoming emotionally over-involved in the child's problem. If the problem belongs to the child, then the parents needs to use strategies that come under parent helping-skills such as listening, acknowledging feelings and problem solving. If the problem belongs to the parent, then the parents need to use discipline strategies or negotiation skills.

Working out who owns the problem is especially useful when you're bringing up teenagers. Sometimes they'll want to make you take on their problems – for example, staying in bed so late that you feel you have to drive them to school or they'll be late.

Here are some examples to illustrate this concept.

- Your child comes home from school upset because their friend wouldn't play with them at playtime – child's problem therefore their needs need meeting first. These are the parent helping-skills of listening, acknowledging feelings and problem solving.
- Your child doesn't want to get dressed when it's time to go out – parents' problem. Parent needs need meeting first, therefore use discipline strategies.
- Your child gets a detention at school for not doing his homework – child's problem, at least initially, and so their needs need meeting first. These are the parent helping skills of listening, acknowledging feelings and problem solving.
- Your child hits his younger sibling – parents' problem and younger sibling problem; therefore discipline strategies and caring for younger sibling.
- Your child is being bullied at school – this could be both the parents' and the child's problem. The parent needs to use parent helping-skills – listening, acknowledging feelings, and problem solving – but also contacting the school to see how they can ensure it doesn't happen again.

EXERCISE

Think about an issue you have with your child. Whose problem is it? And whose needs should be met first?

If parents become emotionally involved in their children's problems, this doesn't always help their children sort out the problem. It is much better to be involved, but not to get too emotional. It's too easy to become entangled and take responsibility for their child's problems. Staying personally involved, as opposed to emotionally involved, encourages a child to grow emotionally and to develop a sense of personal responsibility. It requires trust that the child has the intelligence and ability to solve their problem. Some parents may find it very hard to let their children go and make mistakes because they were not trusted as a child themselves, and so trusting their own children can be very difficult.

Mrs Henderson's Story

Mrs Henderson came to see me about her son's behaviour and her husband's harsh parenting techniques. When I asked what support she was receiving, she told me that she couldn't ask her mother for help as she would get too upset and make the problem worse. It's not only as parents that we need to remain personally involved as opposed to emotionally involved, but also as grandparents too, so that we can support the next generation.

Mrs Pierce and Alice's Story

Mrs Pierce was frustrated that her daughter, Alice, was not getting up in time to walk the mile to school in the morning. This meant that she would be yelling at her daughter to get up, and then they would have to dash to school by car. Mrs Pierce had made a choice to only work part-time, so that she could be at home for her children before and after school. She felt furious and belittled every morning after the rush to get Alice to school.

In the 'Understanding Teenagers' group, she explored how her taking on of her child's problem of being late for school was damaging their relationship. It was also hindering her daughter's growth of maturity and responsibility. With support from the group she told Alice to use her alarm clock, and that she was going to take her dog out for a walk every morning at 8.15 a.m., so would not be available to give her a lift. She told the school she was not going to bring Alice in the car, and that if she was late the school had to handle it themselves. Mrs Pierce was delighted to report back the next week that Alice was taking herself to school on time. She was enjoying her early morning dog walks with her friends.

Remember, if it is your problem you need to use discipline strategies, negotiation or ignoring; but if it's the child's or teenager's problem, you need to use helping skills, such as listening, acknowledging feelings, and help with trying to sort out the problem.

Discipline Strategies: Key Points

★ Discipline means to educate, not to punish. It is an important element of socializing children and teaching them right from wrong.

★ Explicit household rules ensure that children know what's expected of them.

★ Routines give children a sense of security.

★ Limited choice gives children agency without causing too much conflict.

★ The active ignoring of petty undesirable behaviour is a very powerful way to change behaviour, as children like attention.

★ Commands need to be clear, with eye contact and follow-through.

★ Consequences can be natural or logical. They ensure that children grow up understanding that they are responsible for their own behaviour.

★ Star charts, stickers, point systems, marbles in a jar and surprise rewards are all powerful ways of cementing positive behaviours.

★ The 'Four-part Statement' is a positive assertive technique to show your children in a non-blaming way why their behaviour is causing you a problem. Use the following template: 'I feel ... when you ... because ... How can you help me with this problem?'

★ Saying 'No' is an important skill for any parent, and can be done in a firm and loving way.

★ Family meetings are useful forums for discussing family concerns before they become a source of conflict.

★ Negotiation can transform relationships with teenagers. Use the following six-point template: 'I'm concerned when you ... I feel ... I think maybe you feel ... This is what I would like to happen ... What would you like to happen?' Discuss the options, agree a plan of action, monitor the plan.

★ Time Out is useful for 3–8 year olds as a way of exerting control when behaviour has become totally unacceptable – for example, hurting someone or breaking things. Time Out should not be used with older children if they're not used to it, as this will breed more rebellion. It should not be used with children who have attachment issues, such as being fostered or adopted, as it can trigger old memories and make the child very distressed.

★ Problem ownership is a way of deciding what skills to use when there is a problem. If the problem belongs to the child then the parents needs to use the strategies that come under parent-helping skills, such as listening, acknowledging feelings and problem solving. If the problem belongs to the parent, then the parents need to use discipline strategies or negotiation skills.

Chapter 10

Ages and Stages

Understanding ages and stages is really useful when thinking about and managing children's behaviour. If your 18 month-old squirts shampoo all over the bath, you react quite differently than if an eight year-old did the same. The 18 month-old is exploring their environment, whereas the eight year-old may be showing more complex, defiant behaviour.

Your responses have to be appropriate to the child's developmental stage, and expectations of what's acceptable for a child also shift as they get older. Sometimes a parent might feel that their child is doing something deliberately to be naughty, whereas at that age they are incapable of thinking in this manipulative way.

As we grow we go through stages, and each stage is important. The child needs to gain mastery of the developmental tasks of that stage. It can become complicated, though, because children can develop at different rates. A child may be at the appropriate stage for intellectual development, but be at an earlier stage for emotional and social development. This is quite normal. (The stages discussed in this chapter are based on work by Erik Erikson and Clarke and Dawson's book, *Growing up again*; see Appendix 1, 'Stages of psychosocial development', for details.)

The Infant: 0–6 months – Being and Connecting

In the infant phase of development, the baby is not consciously making decisions, but instinctively makes a social connection with their parents from birth. The baby needs to accept and trust the adults who are providing care. It is an adjustment for parents, who have to be on call around the clock. It can seem totally overwhelming.

It is a great change for their couple relationship as well. Many parents, especially mothers, risk becoming depressed around this time, especially if they have felt quite competent in their lives before the baby, but now feel exhausted and unskilled. They may also fall into the trap of feeling that they need to be the perfect parent, which is impossible when you have a baby (being good enough is fine!). Parents need as much support as possible at this time, and family and friends can play a very important role here. Every parent has to learn for the first time how to change the baby's nappy, and how to bathe, dress, feed and burp the baby. This is important. By doing these tasks, parents start to feel more confident in their role, and gradually learn to understand their baby's unique way of responding and communicating with them through crying, expressions and gestures.

As a parent, you'll start to see that the baby has its own unique temperament. The baby feels nurtured by being held, being talked and sung to, and massaged.

Maureen and Zara's Story

Maureen came to see me with her three-month-old baby Zara who was crying all the time. Zara had colic. Maureen found breast-feeding very hard because her baby was often sick – she felt that she didn't know how much she was drinking. Maureen had now changed to bottle-feeding. Her partner was busy working long hours and travelling, so she felt very lonely and isolated.

Maureen was taking Zara to the doctor every week because she felt something was wrong and the baby kept getting colds. Her level of anxiety was sky-high. She had previously had two late miscarriages, and not received any support to deal with the grief from these before becoming pregnant again with this much-wanted baby.

When we worked together, Maureen was able to recognize that her anxiety related to the previous pregnancies. She was able to reduce her worrying about the baby and start to enjoy her – not letting her anxiety over the baby's health stop her playing and forming a bond.

Older Baby and Toddler: 6–18 months – Doing and Exploring

In this stage, the baby is exploring the world by grabbing, pulling, pushing, tasting and putting into their mouths anything that will fit! Babies are beginning to explore their world, learning to trust their senses and be active. The house needs to be child-proofed at this stage, as otherwise your active baby could find and try to drink disinfectant or pull the TV down on themselves before you have time to get out of your chair.

Babies at this stage will repeat doing the same actions again and again until they feel confident in their new skills or they feel they understand. They'll initiate new activities and concentrate while they gain mastery over them. Toddlers love repetitive games, even if this means throwing the plate off the high-chair for the twentieth time and you having to pick it up every time.

Toddlers have no concept of danger, so they need to be kept safe while being able to feel that it's wonderfully exciting to explore their world. Discipline at this stage (for example, if the toddler pulls a cat's tail) is about using distraction or saying 'no' in a quiet voice with eye contact at the same level as your toddler.

Kemi's Story

Kemi came to see me because her 15 month-old toddler was sending her into despair. She had been very house proud, enjoying having everything organized and predictable. The chaos that her son created at home filled her with horror. She was always saying 'no', and thought that her son was intentionally trying to manipulate her by not doing what he was told.

On exploring Kemi's own childhood, we discovered that she had had very rigid parents and that her life had been very controlled. She had then developed anxiety around keeping the home clean. Working with Kemi on this anxiety, she started to feel that she didn't need to be in total control in order to feel safe. She then began to feel much more able to cope with the chaos and energy that a 15 month-old can bring to a family, and even started to enjoy the sheer exuberance of her toddler.

Toddler: 18 Months to 3 Years – Thinking

Many parents call this stage the 'Terrible twos', but I am always excited by this period because it means the child is learning to be independent and their own person, with their own wishes and needs. They need to be able to express anger if they cannot get their own way, slowly learning that they're not the centre of the universe by experiencing the consistent boundaries of their parents. Toddlers can experience raw emotions which can feel overwhelming to them, and they do not have the capacity to put all these feelings into words. Parents have to try to put words to their feelings and thoughts. They also need to be careful not to get drawn into an argument trying to be rational, which will only end up with everyone feeling upset.

In this stage, parents have to set reasonable limits and enforce them because they can be sure their child will be pushing against them. The child will feel much happier if there are consistent and fair rules. The child is realising that they can have an impact on the world, and that there is cause and effect. When your toddler insists that they watch their favourite cartoon on TV yet again, you may feel like screaming. However, the skill is to try not to get angry but to be patient, distracting and acknowledging the desire even as you refuse it. For example – 'You want to watch Fireman Sam again, but it's bedtime now'; or show your toddler a different game or toy that could excite their interest.

For discipline purposes at this stage, it is often better to give your toddler simple clear instructions they can follow and then give descriptive praise for completing the task. Stickers can also be used, because toddlers often find them motivating.

The child can also now start to think about feelings, verbalize them, and imagine other people's feelings. It's therefore useful to teach children options for expressing feelings, such as speaking and drawing, and by giving them the right vocabulary of feeling-words.

Emma's Story

Portia and Boris came to see me because their three year-old daughter, Emma, was getting into trouble at nursery for hitting other children, and was on the verge of being asked to leave.

Portia was devastated. She felt embarrassed and guilty, as Emma was at nursery full-time. She discovered that the nursery staff called Emma the 'the monster' as a joke. I worked with both Portia and the nursery to help Emma relate to her peers in a gentler manner and to stop the nursery from labelling her. I encouraged Portia to spend some time doing child-led play with Emma at the weekend and also a couple of times during the week.

Portia used descriptive praise and gave a sticker to Emma on the days when she'd played gently (no hitting!) with the other children in her nursery.

I worked with the nursery and we instigated Emma getting 10 descriptive praises every day, a sticker for 'playing gently' days, and also the use of distraction when they could see that Emma was getting upset and might hit another child. Within six weeks of this new strategy, Emma was no longer the 'monster child' but was managing well at nursery.

Pre-schooler: 3-6 Years old – Identity and Power

At this stage the child is developing an individual identity. They are engaging in fantasy play, trying out different roles, and asking how? why? when? what? They're learning what it's like to be a little boy or girl. Children at this age often love wearing spiderman, princess, superhero or fireman outfits and many others, as it encourages their imaginative play as they explore different identities and roles. They are also learning about power, how they can use it over other people, and how they can behave in a socially appropriate way. They need firm boundaries, or they could become too powerful and then frightened of their own power. They're also beginning to discover co-operative play.

Stuart's Story

Gloria came to see me because four year-old Stuart was having horrendous tantrums if he didn't get his own way. She seemed scared of him, telling me that Stuart ruled the house. He slept in bed with his mother and would not let his father get into bed with them. Gloria said it was easier that way; at least everyone got a bit of sleep. Not surprisingly this was not helpful for the marital relationship.

The whole family routine and activities were dependent on Stuart. If he wanted to go out to the park, they went out. If he wanted to stay at home, they all stayed home because he had such a tantrum if he didn't get his way.

This age group needs strong boundaries. The father also has to communicate to Stuart that he is the person who stays in the marital bed, not his son. (One job of the father is to reclaim his wife back from his son after all the maternal care-giving, and then establish a good father–son bond.)

Samantha's Story

Samantha came to see me because she was screaming so much at her five year-old daughter who was being defiant about everything, whether it was to get in the car seat, eating her breakfast or putting her shoes on.

Samantha's own childhood had been very abusive. Her parents fought all the time, and her father expected immediate obedience. On exploring this, we were able to see that, on some level, when Samantha saw her daughter she was seeing herself. She would get upset that she had never been able to ever stand up for herself when she was a child. She also felt terrified that she was losing control when her child didn't do what she wanted, so she over-reacted and responded with fury. After looking at her own patterns and her own family script she was able to get in touch with her more loving and curious side, and able to build a much healthier relationship with her daughter.

Primary School Child: 6–12 years – Structure

During this stage, the child wants to have rules, and the freedom that comes from having appropriate rules. This is also a time when the child is intent on learning, and school is very important. The child has to listen to the teachers and to think, practise new skills and learn about responsibility. They will compare themselves to others, attach themselves to a peer group, and experience the consequences of breaking rules.

The child will often challenge parental views but will respect strongly maintained parental authority. The child needs to know that you still love them, even when their behaviour is at times inappropriate. It's helpful at this stage if parents can find one area that their child does well or enjoys, and then support them in this activity – whether it is sport, music, acting, or anything else. This is a time when creativity, imagination and curiosity can flourish. In this stage, children love board games and will be careful to follow all the rules to the end, getting very frustrated if the rules are broken.

Peter's Story

Peter lived half the time in his mum and dad's houses. The separated parents had very different rules around bedtime, TV/screen time and appropriate language. His mother found Peter very difficult to manage, often ending up by screaming at him.

Peter was eight years-old, and came to me as a very confused, angry young boy. He was unpopular in school. He had no friends as he lacked the social skills necessary for making them. I helped him come to terms with his parents' divorce and the feelings of anger and despair he felt from this event. We also worked on friendship issues at school.

However, it was then important to get both his parents together to discuss appropriate boundaries and household rules for both homes. This was important for him to feel safer and that he was not living in two separate worlds. We made a book that he could take between the two houses, in which each parent wrote about what they'd been doing. This also helped Peter to feel he could talk about both his parents in both homes. Peter slowly started to make a friend at school, was able to keep to the rules in both his homes, and become happier in himself.

Peter's parents had to grow themselves, in order to put their child first and try to not let the animosity between them hurt their son's development going through this crucial stage.

Adolescence: 12–18 – Identity, Sexuality and Separation

During this phase, the task of the adolescent is to emerge as an independent, separate person with their own identity and values. They need to be responsible for their own needs, behaviour and feelings. They also need to integrate sexuality into their identity. An adolescent has so many different changes to deal with, that it can be very bewildering for them and for their parents. They have to cope with body changes, educational pressure, social media, their sexuality, body image, peer pressure, trying to find their identity and values, and also be able to separate from their parents.

I often think of adolescence as three developmental stages: the early stage from 12 to 14, a mid-stage from 14 to 16, and then 17–19, each of which has clearly defined characteristics and developmental tasks.

In early adolescence, young people are struggling with new and sometimes painful feelings about themselves and their bodies. This makes them emotionally volatile, as they were when toddlers. One minute they are independent, the next they want to be cuddled and nurtured. They have overwhelming emotions but are not sure how to handle them. These young adults get more excited about starting new projects than finishing them. For people in early adolescence, a close relationship with their same-sex parent can be useful in helping them feel secure during this phase.

In mid-adolescence this process continues. Young people can seem reasonable but then suddenly rebellious. They may want to practise new identities. They may spend a lot of time in their own room, experience mood swings, and not be wanting their parents to get involved in their life. They may want to take risks. They will probably get very interested in their sexuality, but also bewildered and sometimes uncertain about these feelings. This is normal for this stage. They also want to have fun, which could involve alcohol and drug-taking. As the hormone in boys, testosterone, is increasing dramatically, sport, music, dance and other activities can be useful as a way of directing all that energy in a healthy direction. For girls, activities that they enjoy and can gain self-esteem from, such as sport, music, dance, outdoor activities, drama and many others, are also enormously important to help them develop resilience and self-confidence.

Young people can become more reflective as they adjust to the changes in themselves, but the challenges do continue.

Matthew's Story

Lola came to see me because she felt devastated by the loss of her relationship with her son, Matthew, which had been very close. He didn't want to speak to her about his day at school, about his friends, or about his hopes. He would be unjustifiably angry with her if they'd run out of milk or bread. If she asked Matthew questions about his personal life, he became furious and told her to stop interfering in his life.

Through the counselling, Lola began to understand that Matthew was going through an appropriate developmental task of separating from his mother. He, too, found this difficult, accounting for his getting so cross over minor issues. Lola was reassured that she needn't to take it personally, and that often the relationship is restored after this turbulent period in adolescence.

In late adolescence, young people are often thinking more about their future and developing the capacity to form an intimate relationship. They're beginning to have a greater understanding of who they are. They may find separating from their families difficult, and entering a new phase of their life can seem exciting but also daunting. During adolescence, most discipline is gained from negotiation. Sometimes, though, the parent may have to set strong boundaries if the teenager is making dangerous choices, or showing a lack of consideration for the needs of others.

In conclusion, this chapter helps parents understand that parenting has to match the developmental stage of the child. Expecting a two year-old to understand complex reasons why they can't stay up late is too confusing; routine and strong boundaries are more appropriate. However, having rigid bedtimes for a 15 year-old at the weekend when they want to go out with their friends can just breed rebellion.

Ages and stages: Key Points

Child development is a process of stages that children go through. Stages help parents to know what to expect and what to do. In each of the stages, a child has to gain mastery over particular developmental growth tasks.

★ *Infant, 0–6 Months: Connecting and Being.* The parent has to nurture, love and care for the baby. Much of the loving and nurturing comes through tending to the physical needs of the baby.

★ *Older Baby and Toddler, 6–18 Months: Doing and Exploring.* The parent needs to support and encourage the child in their explorations and keep them safe.

★ *Toddler, 18 Months to 3 Years: Thinking.* During this stage the toddler is understanding cause and effect. They are beginning to become their own person with strong wants and desires. The parent needs to give them loving care and set limits.

★ *Pre-schooler, 3–6 Years: Identity and Power.* During this phase, the child is forming their identity and learning what it is to be a boy or girl. They love fantasy-play and are learning about power. Parents need to give loving care and provide strong boundaries.

★ *Primary School, 6–12 Years: Structure.* During this phase, children love structure and rules. They can be a joy to teach, as they have such curiosity about the world. They want everything to be fair. As a parent, it's important to help stimulate their thirst for knowledge and creativity, and to have strong boundaries in which the child can flourish.

★ *Adolescence, 12–18 Years: Identity, Sexuality and Separation.* This phase is a time of great change as the young person becomes an adult with their own identity and values. They have to cope with body changes, educational pressure, peer pressure, social media, their own sexuality and also separate themselves from their parents.

   Parents need to be sensitive to their teenagers' needs, and to listen and be able to negotiate, but also be able to set limits if they feel that their behaviour could be dangerous, or not take into account the needs of others.

Chapter 11

Communication

People build relationships by communication with each other. This chapter describes how to do this successfully and avoid the common pitfalls we so often fall into when trying to communicate with our children. For parents and children to be able to communicate honestly and openly with each other lays the foundation for healthy relationships. This can carry forward to the next generation, and is an enormous gift to give your children.

Communication is much more than just talking. We communicate more with our expression, touch, gestures, posture, tone and volume of voice than with the actual words we use. When we listen, we're not only hearing what the person is saying, we're also interpreting and understanding what their speech conveys. Listening skills can be divided into three clusters:

- Attending skills
- Following skills
- Reflecting skills

Attending Skills

Attending means giving someone your physical attention, with an engaged body posture and eye contact. When I teach listening skills in parenting classes, I'm always fascinated by the fact that the pairs doing a listening exercise will often mirror each other's position when listening to each other. I often ask people to stop what they're doing and just look round the room. The parents observe that most couples are unconsciously mirroring each other's body language. This body matching is a way of communicating acceptance and a willingness to help.

Eye contact is interesting because in some cultures, eye contact between a younger person and an adult is regarded as rude, and is not encouraged. It's important, therefore, to be aware of cultural differences when thinking about eye contact. Some adolescents don't like the pressure of feeling they have your full attention, so on a walk or car journey – when you can talk but it's not too intense as you're both looking ahead – can be a great time to get adolescents to speak with you.

Graham's Story

I was facilitating a 'Living with Teenagers' group where Graham was upset that he didn't seem able to communicate with his son. When he did the listening exercise with his partner, he closed his eyes, becoming very still and leaning back in the chair. His partner felt belittled because she felt that he wasn't listening to her. When challenged, Graham said he always closes his eyes and becomes still when listening to his son because then he can concentrate on what's being said. He hadn't realised that this was perceived by his son as being dismissive and uninterested.

When he put into practice the listening skills learned on the course during the following weeks, he was thrilled to report that he had been able to listen to his son's concerns about deciding which A-levels to do, and that his son had appreciated this.

When you're attending to your child, not paying attention to any distractions is very important. If your mobile phone is ringing all the time or you're looking at messages or the TV, a child will feel that their conversation isn't important and will stop talking with you.

Remember, we communicate far more with our bodies and the way we use our voices than with our words alone. Any words of acceptance will be meaningless to your child if your body is sending the message that you're too busy to be bothered with them right now.

It's also important to think about the other person when you're listening to them. You have to stop thinking about your shopping list or all the list of things you have to do later in the day. Both adults and children pick up very quickly if they're on the receiving end of 'fake listening', and it's very upsetting.

EXERCISE

This exercise has two sections, A and B.

A: In a pair, try to listen badly to your partner for two minutes, look up in the sky, do your shoe laces, look in your handbag, and so on. After this time ask your partner how it felt.

B: The second part of the exercise is for the listener to really listen – silently, saying nothing, and really concentrating on communicating acceptance and understanding while making best efforts to let the speaker know that they care about what they're saying.

The listener and the talker could then swap roles and repeat both A and B. The pair can then tell each other how it felt to be listened to and also just to listen. Did they feel they had to hold back? Did they give full attention and were they aware of the power of silence?

This exercise can be a real 'light-bulb moment' for parents as they see the importance of really listening, and how their partner will often open up and speak about what is concerning them after five minutes of listening. So many of the parents in parenting groups say that they've never experienced good listening before, and what a difference it makes to how they feel.

Following Skills

Many parents divert attention from what the child is saying by asking lots of questions to find out information to sort out the problem. The parent may feel that they're being helpful.

However, this doesn't help the child feel listened to, and they may feel overwhelmed, and won't ask for help again.

'Door-openers' act as a way of encouraging your child to talk, but in a way that's not intimidating. Use sentences like, 'You look as if you had a difficult day – do you want to talk about it?' ... I'm here if you want to talk ... If you want to talk later I'll be here'. Minimal encouragers such as 'Oh ... I see ... sure ... gosh' are also useful to show the child that you're listening to them.

Infrequent open questions can also be useful in keeping a conversation moving. The most important aspect of open questions is to leave the power with the child and not to try to direct them. Questions shouldn't be used by the parent to gather information so that they can come to the best solution and sort out the child's problems, because this doesn't demonstrate really listening to the child. It's an example of taking away control. Open questions help children to open up and share their feelings. Examples of open questions are, 'What happened? ... What was that like?'.

Closed or too-specific questions often only get a 'yes' or 'no' response, and completely control the direction of communication. Examples of closed questions are, 'Did you get into trouble again today? ... What did you do at school today?'. These easily lead to parents just asking one question after another, with the child saying, 'I don't know ... don't remember' in a monotone voice. Information is much more forthcoming in a more general conversation, including also telling your child about your day, for example.

Focused silence is important in helping children talk. Silence gives the child or teenager more time to go deeper into themselves and to experience their feelings. As a parent it can be difficult to have silences because of our own disquiet with this, and so parents will often ask questions or give advice in order not to experience this discomfort. If the parent can really attend to the young person's body posture and non-verbal communication, and think about what they may be feeling, then it's much easier to remain silent and focused on your child while they try to explore their thoughts or feelings.

Simon, Stacey and Susannah's Story

Stacey and Susannah were furious with their father Simon for separating from their mother and starting a new relationship. They hadn't forgiven him after five years, even though he was their main carer, as their mother had mental health issues. During the sessions it turned out that they were most upset because they felt he didn't listen to them. We worked on listening skills for all the family, and soon the relationships became much more constructive.

Reflecting Skills

Reflective listening helps to communicate understanding and acceptance. This can help the child gain insight and get to the core of the issue. In reflective listening you summarize in your own words what you've just heard, as well as the speaker's underlying feelings. The effect of reflective listening is to increase the speaker's self-esteem, to give a powerful message of acceptance, and to encourage the child to take responsibility and develop their own capacity to make decisions.

Reflective listening provides a feedback loop so the listener knows that they've listened correctly. When we listen to another person properly, there are four stages in the process. First, the speaker has the thought, then they put the thoughts into words, the words are heard by the listener, and are then interpreted by combining the words, context and non-verbal communication to give meaning to the communication. Reflective listening is a means of ensuring that the communication doesn't get lost in any of these four stages.

In many ways, problems are like onions with many layers, but with only the top one showing. Often the problem the child talks about is not the real one – for example, They might say 'I hate school', whereas the real problem could be, 'I find it difficult to make friends'. This is why children can sometimes remain upset after their parents think they've solved the problem (for example, by moving school) because this wasn't the underlying problem.

Reflective listening is an enormously useful skill when a child is emotionally upset. When a child is upset they can experience feelings of being completely flooded by emotion, unable to stop these powerful feelings from causing damage – either by being violent or by saying hurtful things. When someone is upset in this way, it can take 20 minutes for the mind to calm down and be rational again.

The following diagram shows what happens in the brain when a child gets flooded with emotions.

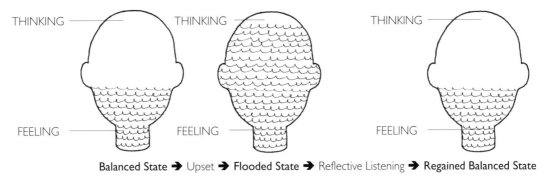

Balanced State ➜ Upset ➜ **Flooded State** ➜ Reflective Listening ➜ **Regained Balanced State**

An Emotionally Flooded Child's Brain

By acknowledging the feeling and reflective listening, you're able to bring the child down to a more balanced state.

Hugh and Kim's Story

Hugh told me that his daughter, nine year-old Kim, had been very upset when her hamster was ill. She was crying when he came in to vacuum-clean her room. She told him that he didn't care that the hamster was ill, and would disturb it by making a noise with the vacuum-cleaner. Hugh got annoyed with Kim, saying that her room needed cleaning. She then asked when Mummy was coming home, to which he replied that she only wanted to complain to mummy to tell her that he was a bad father. This started a massive argument, ending with Kim in tears.

We tried to look at the incident from a new perspective to see what could have been done to avoid such a painful argument. Hugh realised that if he'd used reflective listening, saying things like, 'I know you must be feeling very worried about your hamster who means so much to you', 'You're worried that the noise of the vacuum cleaner could upset your hamster', or 'It's horrible when you feel so helpless to look after your hamster when he's not well'. These comments would have shown Kim that her father did care and was aware of her feelings. I'm sure if he had said any of these statements, he'd have been able to vacuum-clean, and the evening would have progressed without this massive argument.

When emotionally flooded, children become overwhelmed by their feelings. They need help to regain the ability to find their own solutions, while at the same time needing space to express their feelings. The best way to do this is to acknowledge the feelings and help them work them through. By having their emotions validated, children learn that these are natural, and that they can do something about them instead of letting them build up inside. Sometimes all that's required is to name the feeling you're picking up from your child – for example, 'I notice you're feeling cross, frustrated and so on'.

When talking to parents, I use an analogy of a mother bird digesting a worm and feeding it to her fledglings as being like a parent trying to find the right word for the emotion to feed back to their child, so that they can start to regulate their own feelings.

Find a partner to practise reflective listening for five minutes and then change roles. Try to use a difficulty or problem you're actually struggling with, and see if you feel any different after five minutes. Think about whether it's difficult or easy to listen reflectively, and how you could develop this skill.

Michael and Tiffany's Story

Michael and Tiffany came to see me because their three children – aged 11 and a pair of seven year-old twins – were being violent to each other, and rude and aggressive to their parents. During the interview I realised that Michael and Tiffany didn't seem able to communicate with each other. They weren't able to listen or understand what their partner had said. I used a technique from couple therapy in which one member of the couple talks for five minutes while the partner just has to listen and reflect back what they've heard. They're not allowed to answer or come back with any questions or denials. This is to ensure that the speaker knows that the listener has really heard what they've said. After the five minutes is up, the roles are switched and the other partner speaks.

It became clear during this exercise that Michael and Tiffany had never been able to discuss a coherent way to parent their children, or to agree on any boundaries or rules, because they didn't want to listen to each other. By challenging the parents to do this, they were able to discuss some difficult issues, including the differences in their parenting styles, to try to come to a decision about how to parent their children. In due course, after numerous sessions they did come up with some boundaries and had learned the skills to enforce them. When the children saw that their parents were working together, their behaviour also became much more controllable.

Problems in Communications

Communication (both listening and talking) is complex. I often wonder how people manage to stay in any relationship, because it's so complex and very few people are taught to communicate successfully. I sometimes feel that in order to survive with a family, we all need an honours degree in emotional literacy and communication skills.

When we talk to someone, there are three different categories of unhelpful responses. These have been adapted from a book called *People Skills* by Robert Bolton (1986).

1. Judgemental Responses, Such as Criticising and Labelling

Parents often criticize their child because they think this will make them work harder, be kinder, and be more thorough. However, it often has the opposite effect, making the child downhearted. Other, more encouraging techniques described in this book actually prove more effective at changing behaviour.

Zac's Story

Zac was 15 and had given up studying. His parents criticized him all the time, saying he was playing too much on his computer, he wasn't revising enough, he didn't have the right type of friends. Both his parents had very harsh upbringings. They were trying so hard to make him successful that they didn't realise that these judgemental responses were destroying his sense of self-worth. Both Zac and his parents came to family therapy to help them to develop a positive relationship and to stop the communication patterns being so judgemental.

Taking control, by telling children what to do all the time, makes them resistant and resentful, and also destroys self-esteem. Some parents feel tempted to tell their children what they should or ought to do in every single situation. This increases the child's anxiety, and in the long run breeds rebellion. Giving advice all the time can also disempower the child. It's much better for them to make their own decisions, and advising may imply some contempt for the child's own abilities to sort out their own problems. Of course, if you're really asked for advice by your child, it's fine to offer it.

2. Avoiding the Child's Concerns Prevents Any Real Communication

Reassurance doesn't reassure because you're not really hearing the child. Thus when Angela says, 'I'm really stupid at reading', to say 'No, you're not, you can read some difficult books and the other girls in your class are all super bright', doesn't improve how Angela feels. It's far better to listen properly and try to appreciate what your child is saying and feeling – for example, by saying 'You're really worried about your reading, aren't you?'. By insisting that she's a good reader means she's not being heard or witnessed.

Jonas' Story

Jonas was scared at the idea of going to secondary school. He was having nightmares and he was behaving badly at home. He was refusing to do his chores and was barely doing his homework. His parents came to see me because they were concerned that their normally happy child seemed to have suddenly changed to become angry, defiant and tearful.

When we explored what was happening, Jonas explained clearly that he was nervous of going to a new secondary school as all his friends were going to a different school. His parents were at first dismissive of his concerns, saying the new school was excellent and he'd have lots of new opportunities there. He could take up a new instrument because it had an excellent orchestra. They told him not to be silly because he'd love the new school and make new friends quickly. Jonas remained sullen in the session and refused to speak.

After two individual sessions with Jonas I realised his concerns about the new school were very real, and he felt that his parents were being dismissive of them. In a review session with his parents Jonas explained his concerns and his parents then took them seriously and arranged for Jonas to visit the school three times, and they made contact with another family with a son going to the school. A play-date was arranged for the two boys and they enjoyed playing together. Jonas then became much happier as he felt his concerns had been properly listened to and that he was not just receiving empty reassurance.

3. Diverting or Distracting

These are classic ways of changing a conversation to a topic you want to talk about or feel more comfortable with, meaning the child isn't heard. Logical reasoning is another way of withdrawing from a difficult emotion – once again, the child won't feel heard or witnessed.

Elizabeth's Story

Mr and Mrs Taylor came to see me because they were worried their daughter Elizabeth aged 14 was becoming more and more reclusive.

They lived in the countryside in a small cottage, and Elizabeth found friendships difficult and didn't enjoy going to her secondary school. She felt like an outsider, and wasn't in any of the 'popular girl groups'. She spent a lot of time in her bedroom.

Both the Taylors had experienced a tough upbringing and had worked since they were 14 years of age. They had Elizabeth when they thought they could no longer have children, and saw her as a great blessing.

Elizabeth was desperate to have a dog as a companion but her father was adamant that it would be too expensive and time consuming to look after, which left Elizabeth feeling completely rejected, and so she withdrew more into herself. This in turn left her parents feeling furious and worried because they felt that she should act more 'grown up' and just accept their decision. They tried to get her interested in their local church youth club and the girl guides.

Elizabeth was not interested in either of these diversions.

I worked with Elizabeth for six weeks, and we devised a plan to try and persuade her parents to let her have a dog. (I gained the permission of her parents for this, as I didn't want to undermine them.) Elizabeth's mother was more accepting of the idea but felt she had to support her husband.

The plan involved making a power-point presentation in our sessions to persuade her parents that a dog would be a positive addition to the household.

She wrote down all the positives, and addressed her father's issues by saying she would pay for the dog by getting a job doing a paper round, and that she'd walk the dog before and after school. Elizabeth spent a lot of time researching the best breed of dog for them to welcome into the family.

On the review meeting, Elizabeth showed the power-point presentation to her parents, who started to see her point of view and were impressed by all the work she'd done. They decided to get a retired guide dog for the blind.

I saw Elizabeth and her family two months later and was delighted that the whole family were enjoying the dog, Elizabeth was much happier in school, and she'd found a friend who enjoyed walking dogs as well. Elizabeth was no longer having her wishes rejected, and had reconnected with a warm loving relationship with her parents again.

Communication: Key Points

★ Communication is more than just talking; much of our communication is non-verbal.

★ Listening skills can be divided into three categories: attending, following and reflecting.

★ Reflective listening means to reflect back the feeling and paraphrase the content.

★ The results of reflective listening are increased self-esteem, feeling accepted, and having a greater confidence in making your own decisions.

★ Problems in communication can be caused by responses which are either judgemental, assert control, or are not really listening to the child's concerns.

Chapter 12

Stress Management

All parents would agree that at times, parenting can be immensely stressful. Managing stress so we do not damage our closest relationships is essential. This chapter looks at stress management from both the parent's and child's perspective. Parents can learn how to manage their stress and give calmer responses. Children can learn different ways of reacting to stress rather than by lashing out, having temper-tantrums or withdrawing into themselves.

Stress management is a way of becoming aware of our own feelings by thinking about the physical sensations we're having. This helps to stop us from reacting unthinkingly to events. Many parents are not aware of the level of stress we're under, and then crack when something quite minor happens because it puts us 'over the edge'. Having children is simply very stressful, so if we're also working, and have financial worries or other family problems, life can seem very demanding.

By becoming more aware of the physical sensations in our body we have a measure of how stressed we are, helping us to think about how to dispel the stress. I notice myself that when I get stressed, my right eyelid begins to tremor, I start to be a little irrational and bad-tempered, and feel my heart rate increase.

EXERCISE

Think about the physical sensations that you have with the following feelings: anger, sadness, being scared, frustrated, irritated, happy, excited. This will help raise the physical awareness of where and how we feel emotions in our bodies – for example, 'When I feel worried, I get a sick feeling in my stomach and my mouth goes dry'. This help us to understand the occasions and situations when we feel these emotions.

Daphne and Mary's Story

Daphne came to see me because she was finding her teenage daughter Mary very difficult. Daphne had recently lost her mother, had been through a painful divorce, and felt very vulnerable and isolated. She had a job that was stressful and responsible, and worked long hours. When we discussed the amount of stress she was under, Daphne was able to understand that she was losing her temper very quickly because stress meant she had a short fuse. For example, when her daughter didn't tidy her room when asked or didn't answer her, she felt overwhelming anger.

From her sessions with me, Daphne was able to see that she needed to do something to help manage her stress. She decided to start running, which she'd enjoyed when she was much younger. This small change helped her control her stress, and enabled her to use other strategies to heal the relationship with her daughter.

In my sessions with parents who are very stressed, I make the analogy of a bottle with a cork in it filled up with lots of feeling from the day – for example, could not find my key to the car (frustrated), the battery in my phone was flat (annoyed), my boss said my presentation was poor (angry), my children made me late for work because they weren't ready (fuming), the train was delayed (exhausted), and then when finally your partner tells you they have to work late, the cork comes out as you explode with fury.

One way of stopping this build-up of emotion is to let the feelings out slowly throughout the day – for example, telephoning a friend to say you're having an awful day. Some people find mindfulness exercises or concentrating on their breathing can help them remain calm.

When I work with children, they often have anger issues at school and home. To tackle this, I sometimes draw an iceberg with the feeling of anger above the water. When we dive below the water-line of the iceberg, however, we often find lots of other feelings which are fuelling the anger – these can be shame, fear, guilt, frustration, jealousy, loss and hurt.

Jim's Story

Jim lashed out at home against his younger sister and his parents. They were very angry and worried about him. When we did the iceberg drawing, Jim was able to say that beneath the feeling of anger was jealousy of his sister because she seemed much preferred by his parents. He'd also had a bad day at school because his best friend had told him he didn't want to play with him any longer. He felt stupid, too, because he couldn't understand what his teacher was telling him to do for homework. When his sister had then taken his favourite cuddly toy, he couldn't bear it and lashed out.

By doing this exercise, Jim was able to understand his emotions more, realising that while the emotion is valid, you can't behave violently but need to find another way to express how you feel.

With children who are often angry, it can be useful to see when they're angry and in what circumstances, and to remember what happened beforehand and the consequences afterwards. This provides information about possible triggers for the anger – such as the time, the person, the environment or the task that the child was supposed to do – and the consequences, such as getting their own way, feeling powerful or watching an enormous row blow up between their parents.

With anger in adults, there might be other feelings under the surface – for example, a father who's furious at his child who had hidden from him for 20 minutes in the park. This fury is masking total relief that his child has been found safely. Another example is a mother angry with her daughter for not telling her about how well she did at school, which could be masking feelings of shame that her daughter isn't communicating with her.

Ravindu and Janani's Story

Ravindu came to see me with his daughter Janani. They'd had a furious row over a broken arrangement to go to the cinema together. The intensity of their fight had shaken him. When we analysed what was going on by using the iceberg drawing, we saw what other emotions lay beneath the fury caused by Janani not coming to the cinema with her father. Ravindu felt misunderstood, taken for granted, hopeless and disappointed since he'd wanted it to be a big treat. He had a stressful job and was aware that he'd not given as much time to Janani as he'd have liked, so he also felt guilty. Janani was upset and angry at the top of her 'iceberg', but underneath were feelings of being misunderstood, scared and worried about her revision, which was why she'd cancelled going out with her father.

By doing this exercise they were both able to get a better understanding of each other, and their relationship started to heal.

Using the image of a thermometer as a guide, it is crucial to realise that if you're red-hot at 100 degrees, then you'll respond in an unthoughtful way, and it makes much more sense to respond in a calm way when your own thermometer has gone down to 50 degrees. This can stop situations escalating in unhelpful ways.

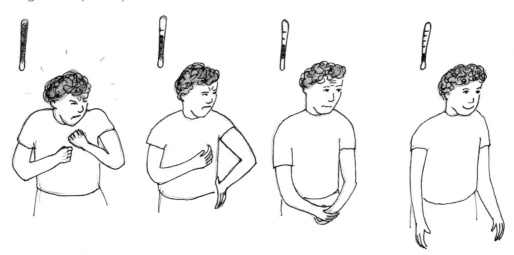

Sometimes even with very empathic parenting our children's behaviour can be very confusing and difficult to understand. In these cases going to your doctor to get advice or a referral to an appropriately qualified therapist for an assessment and intervention could be very helpful in giving you more guidance on how to manage your child's behaviour. Feeling supported in this way can also serve to reduce the stress.

It is also helpful to think about what triggers our anger and why this is so. The reasons could lie deep in our own family script from past generations. Some ways of relieving anger are exercise, listening to music, using visualizations, reading, a special scent, or cooking, for example. We all have our own anger-busters which are useful to deploy so that we don't unintentionally destroy relationships.

Our physical health is intimately connected to our emotional health, so it's important to try and stay physically well. Sometimes if you're feeling down, if you decide to stand up tall, breath deeply and put your shoulders back, just these small adjustments can improve how you feel and think.

Stress Management: Key Points

★   Awareness of our body's physical sensations helps us to understand our feelings.

★   Stress affects how we react to events.

★   Letting feelings out slowly can stop an explosion of angry feelings.

★   Anger often masks other feelings such as fear, shame and hurt.

★   Use the image of a thermometer to imagine your emotional level – if your 'temperature' is very high, wait until you've cooled down before responding.

★   It's useful to think about what triggers your anger and if the reasons for this are still relevant.

★   Finding your own ways of reducing anger is important – for example, exercise, music, reading, talking to a friend.

Conclusion

It is only recently that we have understood that it takes skill and expertise to raise children to be happy, caring, confident and capable adults. For any other complex task of this importance, we'd be reaching for a thick manual. Parenting can bring huge joy, love and excitement, but it also can bring worry, anger and sadness.

My dream is for all parents from every race, culture, class and religion to have access to all these skills to develop children who are caring, with a strong sense of who they are and sound mental health. As a society, I would like us to be able to ensure that all parents can get the benefits of this information by whatever means possible – the web, parenting courses or books.

For some parents the skills described in this book will be like a new language, but for the children who are brought up by parents using these skills, they will then come naturally when they become parents.

In this way, we can hopefully start to have new generations of confident and caring young people. The world will then be a nurturing place, with people who have high self-esteem, are able to love and be loved, and able to co-operate and find unique ways to lead creative, responsible and productive lives.

Thank you for reading this book, and I wish you great joy from your parenting.

Theories that Underpin Parenting Education

In all my work with parents I have found the following theories useful in thinking about parenting interventions which help children grow up as strong and sound adults with a clear identity in their own right. Many of these theories come from the giants of twentieth-century psychology.

The books that are highlighted in bold text are the ones I most often recommend to parents when I'm seeing them for family therapy or parenting work.

Attachment Theory

Attachment theory was conceived by John Bowlby and was a fascinating development from psycho-dynamic theory. It consists of four strands

A. Secure Base

After working with juvenile offenders, Bowlby developed a theory in which the attachment between the primary caregivers and the baby is of the utmost importance. This bond gives the child a secure base from which it can explore the world. An example of this is often played out by toddlers and parents in a park. You commonly see a toddler moving from the bench on which his parents are sitting to explore their surroundings, then looking back to make sure his parents are still there, and then suddenly deciding that they've gone far enough and start running back to them. Developmentally this continues, as the child goes to school and then ventures out into the world on their own. All individuals feel safe and secure when they know they have a loving relationship they can return to: as they get older they'll venture further, but still need to know that their loved ones are available.

B. Internal Working Model

The child also develops a working model of how he is known in the world, from the people who've responded to him in the first five years. If he's been treated with love and patience and smiles, he will feel that the world loves him. This is transferred to all other relationships: if he has a neutral encounter with someone, he'll expect that person to have liked him. This working model of thinking 'the world loves me and I am lovable' is like a jewelled box that a child can take with him throughout his life, deeply embedded in his psyche.

The converse is also true. If he has been brought up with parents not being warm and caring but angry and dismissive of his feelings, then when he has a neutral encounter he'll expect that person not to like him, and his behaviour will often ensure that they don't.

C. Sensitive Responsiveness

Nurturing parenting is about being sensitive to your child's small nuances of behaviour and responding to these. It's about reading the signs that your child is giving you – e.g. do they want a cuddle or do they want to play; are they hungry or tired? Sensitive responsiveness is a precursor to a child feeling really watched and witnessed so that his sense of reality is confirmed.

D. Trajectories

Bowlby thought that a child's trajectory in life was foretold from when he was very young, i.e. about five years of age, unless an intervention was made to help get him on to a better trajectory. A trajectory of having unsatisfactory relationships and problems as he grows up could be ameliorated by his parents attending a parenting education course, or having counselling themselves when a child is still young.

Mary Ainsworth developed Bowlby's ideas, developing a mechanism to assess the type of attachment a child had to their mother – avoidant, ambivalent or secure.

Pat Crittenden has done further fascinating work elaborating on the theory, and how to intervene productively with parents.

FURTHER READING – Attachment Theory
- Ainsworth, M., Blehar, M., Waters, E and Wall, S. (1978) *Patterns of attachment: A psychological study of the Strange Situation*, Lawrence Erlbaum Associates Hillsdale, NJ.
- Bowlby, J. (1961) *Child care and the growth of love*, Pelican, Harmondsworth.
- Bowlby, J. (1969) *Attachment*, Hogarth Press, London.
- Bowlby, J. (1973) *Separation, anxiety and anger*, Hogarth Press, London.
- Bowlby, J. (1980) *Loss: sadness and depression*, Hogarth Press, London.
- Bowlby, J. (1988) *A secure base: Clinical applications of attachment theory*, Routledge, London.
- Bowlby, J., Robertson, J. and Rosenbluth, D. (1952) 'A two year old goes to hospital', *Psychoanalytic Studies of the Child*, 7, 82–94.
- Crittenden, P. (2011) *Raising parents*, Taylor and Francis/Willan Publishing, Cullompton, Devon.

The Holding Relationship

Children need to know that they are being held in mind by their parent. This was described by D.W. Winnicott as a 'primary maternal preoccupation' (1956/1958). Perhaps he should have included fathers too. If parents are ill, traumatized, addicts or have themselves received poor parenting, they may find this difficult to do, as they have no internal model to follow of what constitutes a good parent. Winnicott emphasized that parents only need to be 'good enough', not perfect. He also once said 'there is no such thing as a baby' on its own but that it was always in relationship with its main carer, and this provides the basis for all development.

FURTHER READING – The Holding Relationship
- Winnicott, D.W. (1958) *Collected papers: Through paediatrics to psychoanalysis*, Hogarth, London.
- Winnicott, D.W. (1965) *The maturational process and the facilitating environment*, Hogarth, London.
- Winnicott, D.W. (1971) *Playing and reality*, Hogarth, London.

Social Learning Theory

Social learning theory defined human interactions as being dependent on either positive or negative reinforcement. The main architect of this theory was B. F. Skinner. Skinner described this as operant conditioning. When you reward behaviour, that behaviour will continue. Praise, star charts and tangible rewards (as discussed earlier in this book) are examples of positive reinforcement, and can be very useful in getting children to behave appropriately.

Negative reinforcement such as ignoring, consequences and Time Out can also be very useful. However, a word of caution is in order here, because if the child has had a traumatic past or finds the social world difficult to understand, sometimes negative reinforcement can make matters worse. Parenting is an art, not a science, and every child is unique so will need parenting that is tailor-made to their individuality. Recent work by Pink has called into question some of the ideas behind using social learning theory as a motivational force, as it could take away the child's intrinsic motivation. Pink emphasizes the importance of not having an if/then relationship to motivate children, but giving appreciation by surprise rewards.

> ### FURTHER READING – Social Learning Theory
> - Phelan. T.W. (1995) *123 Magic: effective discipline for children 2–12*, ParentMagic Inc., Glen Ellyn, IL.
> - Pink. D.H. (2011) *Drive*, Canongate Books, Edinburgh.
> - **Webster-Stratton. C. (1992) *The incredible years*, Umbrella Press, Chicago.**

Stages of Psychosocial Development

Erik Erikson, who developed this theory, was a social scientist who believed that we pass through a series of developmental stages during our life cycle. Jean Illsey Clarke and Connie Dawson then adapted them in their book *Growing up again* so that as parents, we understand how to support children in every phase. I find them fascinating, as these stages give such unique insight into the emotional world of the child and how to ensure that they don't get fixed at a particular stage.

These stages are illuminating because they set out the essential questions which frame a child's behaviour during the different stages of growing up.

These are the stages described by Clarke and Dawson (1998):

Stage 1 (Being), Birth to 6 Months: is it OK for me to get my needs known and met? Can I trust or mistrust these people to look after me?

Stage 2 (Doing), 6–18 Months: is it OK for me to explore and trust what I learn?

Stage 3 (Thinking), 18 Months – 3 Years: is it OK for me to think for myself? Can I develop autonomy and not doubt myself?

Stage 4 (Identity and Power), 3–6 Years: is it OK to be who I am, to find out who other people are and learn the consequences of my actions? Is it OK to use my initiative?

Stage 5 (Structure), Age 6–12: How do I develop a capacity for industry at school and social competence?

Stage 6 (Identity, Sexuality, Separation), Age 13–19: Is it OK to develop my own values and belong, to be independent and honour my sexuality?

Stage 7 (Interdependence), Adult: is it OK to become interdependent and develop intimacy and love?

FURTHER READING - **Stages of Psychosocial Development**
- Erikson, Eric H. (1959). *Identity and the life cycle*, International Universities Press, Madison, CT.
- Erikson, Eric H. and Joan M. (1997) *The life cycle completed: extended version*, W.W. Norton, New York.
- Illsley Clarke, J. (1978) *Self esteem: a family affair*, Winston, Oak Grove, MN.
- Illsley Clarke,. J. and Dawson, C. (1998) *Growing up again: parenting ourselves, parenting our children*. Hazelden Trade, Center City, MN.

Proximal Development

Lev Vygotsky was a Russian psychologist who studied child development, and coined the idea of a 'zone of proximal development'. A child can be encouraged to learn more in their zone of proximal development by 'scaffolding' learning in small steps so they can reach their full potential. This is true in social education as well as in more cognitive education – for example, schools use social stories in which they imagine a situation and discuss how you could respond to support children learning how to react in different scenarios that have been causing problems.

FURTHER READING – **Proximal Development**
- Schaffer, R. (1996) *Social development*, Blackwell, Oxford.

Psychodynamic Theory

Sigmund Freud developed a theory of the unconscious, the idea that all behaviour has a meaning and sometimes you have to delve into the unconscious to try to understand why a child may behave in the way he does.

Freud (1923) divided the mind into three – the unconscious *id*, our impulsive instinctual side; the *ego*, which mediates between our desires and drives and the demands of the real world; and the *superego*, which incorporates the values and morals of our society and our parents. The idea of the superego can be useful in thinking about how parental influence can be internalized into either a very critical or a more humane superego.

His theory of psychosexual development has been extremely influential in how we understand the development of sexuality in children from infancy onwards.

In her 1975 book *Ghosts in the nursery* Selma Fraiberg describes how memories of our early experiences of being parented can return as 'ghosts', intruding upon our attempts as parents to care for our own children, unless we recognize how these experiences may have stayed with us.

FURTHER READING – Psychodynamic Theory

- Freud, S. (1905/1977) 'Three essays on the theory of sexuality', in *Pelican Freud Library Volume 7: On sexuality*, Penguin, Harmondsworth.
- Freud, S. (1917/1973) *Introductory lecture on psychoanalysis*, Penguin, Harmondsworth.
- Freud, S. (1923/1949) *The ego and the Id*, Standard Edition, 19: Hogarth, London, pp. 1–16.
- Fraiberg, S. (1959) *The magic years*, Charles Scribner's, New York.
- Fraiberg, S. (1975) 'Ghosts in the nursey', *Journal of the American Academy of Child and Adolescent Psychiatry*, 14 (3), 387–421.
- Miller, A. (1979) *The drama of being a child*, Faber and Faber, London.
- Miller, A. (1983) *For your own good: hidden cruelty in child-rearing and the roots of violence*, Faber and Faber, London.

Mentalization

Peter Fonagy, a Professor of Psychoanalysis, has developed a theory of mentalization. The theory proposes that the ability to be able to understand their own and other people's emotional states can determine successful emotional development. Thus, the ability to be able to regulate your own emotions is of great importance in how you parent your children, and if a parent is unable to do this, it could have a negative outcome for the child. The child would find it hard to regulate their own feelings as well as being unable to interpret the feelings of others.

FURTHER READING – Mentalization

- Fonagy, P., Gergely, G., Jurist, E. and Target, M. (2002) *Affect regulation, mentalization and the development of the self*, Other Press, New York.
- **Cooper, A. and Redfern, S. (2016)** *Reflective parenting*, Routledge, Abingdon, Oxon.

Structural Family Therapy

Salvador Minuchin developed the theory of Structural Family Therapy. He regarded it as being of the utmost importance that parents held the authority in the family, and that when things started to go awry it was often because the alliances and boundaries had got muddled up.

He was interested in discovering the family rules, patterns and structures and then unbalancing them in order to develop more healthy systems and communication in the family. Common illustrations of the type of issues with which he worked were when a mother and children became a subset against a more peripheral father, or when a child is given too much power because there's a power vacuum in the parental subsystem and so the child will start to use the power but will also feel very unsafe and unhappy.

> **FURTHER READING – Structural Family Therapy**
> * Minuchin, S. (1974) *Families and family therapy,* Harvard University Press, Cambridge, MA.

Discipline Approaches from Individual Psychology

Dreikurs built on Adler's theory of individual psychology to develop his approach to discipline. His theory states that the reason children misbehave is because they don't feel they belong. When this happens the child is motivated by one of four goals: undue attention-getting, power, revenge and display of inadequacy. The diagnosis of the goals and then the corrective measures – such as natural and logical consequences, family councils etc. – are used to help parents understand and manage their children's behaviour. The aim is that parents are able to help their children co-operate without punishment or reward, and because they feel valued.

> **FURTHER READING – Discipline Approaches (Individual Psychology)**
> * Dinkmeyer, D. Sr., McKay, G. and Dinkmeyer, D. Jr. (1997) *Systemic training for effective parenting,* Step Publishers, Fredericksburg, VA.
> * Dreikurs, R, and Soltz, V. (1991) *Children: The challenge,* Plume/Penguin, New York.
> * Gordon, T. (2008) *Parent effectiveness training,* 30th edn, Three Rivers Press, New York (orig. 1975).

Non-Directive Play

Virginia Axline developed non-directive play therapy, the principles based on Carl Rogers' person-centred psychotherapy approach. She established eight principles of non-directive play therapy. These are: the importance of warmth, acceptance and having the permission of the child to work with them; to be able to reflect back feelings to the child and not to direct their activities or hurry them; and finally to only set limits related to not hurting themselves or others or damaging property.

Rachel Pinney pioneered 'Children's Hours', also known as 'creative listening', in which a child is able to feel totally validated during a non-directive play session. This practice has an enormous impact on a child's self-esteem.

FURTHER READING – Non-Directive Play
- Axiline, V.M. (1947) *Play therapy*, Ballantine Books, New York.
- Axiline, V. (1980) *Dibs: In search of self*, Penguin, Harmondsworth.
- Goldschmied, E. and Jackson, S. (2003) *People under three. Young children in day care*, 2nd edn (Chapter 6, The treasure basket), Routledge, Abingdon, Oxon.
- **James, O. (2012) *Love bombing*, Karnac Books, London.**
- Jenkinson, S. (2001) *The genius of play*, Hawthorn Press, Stroud.
- Pinney, R. (1986) *Bobby: Breakthrough of a special child*, McGraw-Hill, New York.

Communications Approach

Hiam Ginott's books on parenting give excellent guidance on how to ensure that communication between parents and children is in a spirit of mutual respect – for example, making a distinction between the child and the behaviour, offering limited choices and letting children do what they can for themselves.

FURTHER READING – Communications Approach
- **Biddulph, S. (2002) *The secret of happy children*, 3rd edn, Marlowe and Co., New York (orig. 1984).**
- **Ginott, H. (1965) *Between parent and child*, Macmillan, Basingstoke.**
- **Ginott, H. (1969) *Betweeen parent and teenager*, Macmillan, Basingstoke.**
- Faber, A. and Mazlish, E. (1985) *Liberated parents liberated children*, HarperCollins, New York (orig. 1974).
- **Faber, A. and Mazlish, E. (2012a) *Siblings without rivalry: How to help your children live together so you can live too*, Piccadilly Press, London (orig. 1980).**
- **Faber, A. and Mazlish, E. (2012b) *How to talk so kids will listen and listen so kids will talk*, 3rd edn, Piccadilly Press, London (orig. 1982).**
- Gottman, J. (1997) *The heart of parenting: How to raise an emotionally intelligent child*, Simon & Schuster, New York.

Relationship Education

Virginia Satir argued that every child or parent's behaviour was a response to a complex set of rules governing the family group. These rules could be unconscious. By making these patterns of behaviour explicit, they can be understood and changed.

Further Reading – Relationship Education

- Bolton, R. (1986) *People skills: How to assert yourself, listen to others and resolve conflicts*, Simon & Schuster, New York.
- Satir, V. (1989) *The new peoplemaking*, 2nd edn, Science and Behavior Books, Palo Alto, CA.
- Satir, V. (1993) *Conjoint family therapy*, Science and Behavior Books, Palo Alto, CA.

Family Scripts

John Byng Hall was a family therapist who wrote about the impact of family scripts from previous generations on the lives of the present generation. He wrote about family scripts and their significance in our present-day relationships, and how they can be changed by forming corrective scripts as opposed to just replicating them. Family scripts do serve to stabilize a family, as everyone knows what behaviour is expected of them. Therapists sometimes help the family to change the old patterns. Family myths and beliefs are also tied up with the ideas of family scripts and hence their power over future generations.

Further Reading – Family Scripts

- Byng-Hall, J. (1995) *Rewriting family scripts: Improvisation and systems change*, Guilford Press, New York.

Person-Centred Psychotherapy

Carl Rogers developed humanistic psychotherapy, also known as person-centred psychotherapy. He stated that people needed three basic conditions in order to develop as human beings: unconditional positive regard, congruence and acceptance. He thought that if people experienced this, they'd be able to develop their real self and not a false self, and so be able to self-actualize.

Further Reading – Person-Centred Psychotherapy

- Rogers, C. (1961) *On becoming a person: A therapist's view of psychotherapy*, Houghton Mifflin, New York.

Neuroscience

Sue Gerhardt has lead the way in utilizing recent strides forward in our understanding of the brain in terms of the connections between the limbic system and the pre-frontal cortex, in order to think about children whose brains are flooded with stress hormones. Another pioneer in the field, Daniel J. Siegel, has explored the plasticity of the brain and some of the reasons for teenage behaviour.

FURTHER READING – **Neuroscience**
- Gerhardt, S. (2004) *Why love matters*, Brunner-Routledge, Hove, East Sussex (2nd edn, 2015).
- Siegel, D. and Payne Bryson, T. (2011) *The whole brain child*, Robinson, London.
- **Sunderland, M. (2006)** *The science of parenting*, **Dorling Kingsley, London.**

Other Strongly Recommended Books
- Elliott, A. (2013) *Why can't my child behave? Empathic parenting strategies that work for adoptive and foster families*, Jessica Kingsley, London.
- Pentecost, D. (2000) *Parenting the ADD child*, Jessica Kingsley, London.
- Siegel, D. and Hartzell, M. (2003) *Parenting from the inside out*, Tarcher/Penguin, New York.
- Biddulph, S. (1998) *Raising boys*, Thorsons, London.
- Biddulph, S. (2017) *10 Things girls need most*, Thorsons, London.
- Golding, K.S and Hughes, D.A (2012) *Creating loving attachments*, Jessica Kingsley Publishers, London (especially useful for adoptive or foster parents).
- Siegel, D. and Payne Bryson, T (2018) *The yes brain child*, Simon and Schuster.

Resources: Information on Helpful Organizations and Services

This is not an exhaustive list but hopefully it can point you in the right direction. The charity 'Family Lives' has a brilliant website that provides links to many organizations that give support and advice for many different issues.

Part A. For Parents

Adoption
- *Adoption UK:* Provides information, training, guidance and support at all stages of the adoption process; www.adoptionuk.org

Anger Management
- *Anger Management:* Provides information, self-help tips and explains how anger management works; www.nhs.uk/conditions/anger-management

Babies
- *Association for Post Natal Illness:* A charity to support mothers with post-natal depression; www.apni.org
- *Child Accident Prevention Trust:* Advice on Baby & Child safety; www.capt.org.uk
- *Cry-sis:* Provides support and advice regarding excessively crying or sleepless babies; www.cry-sis.org.uk; tel. 08451 228 669.
- *Five to Thrive:* fivetothrive.org.uk – advice on positive parenting with baby based on five ingredients: relax, play, cuddle, respond and talk; www.barnardos.org.uk/baby-workout.pdf
- Health advice and guidelines on helping your baby to sleep, introducing solid foods etc.: www.nhs.uk/conditions/pregnancy-and-baby
- Parent Infant Psychotherapy is available now in some NHS Trusts for parents needing help in their relationship with their infants.

Bereavement
- *Cruse Bereavement Care:* A charity that offers free confidential support to adults and children after the death of someone close. www.cruse.org.uk, Helpline 0808 808 1677.
- *Winston's Wish:* A charity supporting bereaved children and young people; www.winstonswish.org

Bullying
- *Bullying UK:* Part of Family Lives gives information and advice (including by email) to those affected by bullying; www.bullying.co.uk
- *Child Exploitation and Online Protection:* An excellent website with up-to-date advice if you are concerned about internet bullying or your child being inappropriately contacted; www.ceop.police.uk/safety-centre/
- *Kidscape:* They aim to provide children, families, carers and professionals with advice, training and practical tools to prevent bullying. Tel. 0207 730 3300; parent advice line, 0207 823 5430; www.kidscape.org.uk

Children with Special Needs

Contact a Family: Provides advice and support to parents of disabled children; www.cafamily.org.uk, tel. 0808 808 3555.

National Autistic Society: A charity that offers support to parents of autistic children, and also runs seminars, workshops and courses to help parents raise their autistic child, aiming to improve the lives of people with autism in the UK; www.autism.org.uk

Couples

Oneplusone – Thinking Relationships: Helps people build stronger relationships; www.oneplusone.space

Relate: Confidential counselling service for relationship problems of any kind; www.relate.org.uk 0300 100 1234.

Divorce and Separation

Family Mediators Association: A membership organization of family mediators. Their aim is to help parents reach agreements about what should happen after divorce or separation; www.thefma.co.uk

Parent Connection: An organization that supports parenting after parting. www.theparentconnection.org.uk

Parents as Partners: www.tavistockrelationships.org, for parents who are separating when it has a detrimental effect on the children

Drugs

FRANK: provides advice to anyone affected by drugs and substance misuse; www.talktofrank.com, tel. 0300 123 6600.

Fathers

Fatherhood Institute: A research organization providing information on the impact that fathers have on babies, children and mothers; www.fatherhoodinstitute.org

Grandparents

Grandparents Plus: A national charity working for all families where grandparents play a vital role in the development of their grandchildren. Advice line 0300 123 7015l www.grandparentsplus.org.uk

Helplines

* *Childline:* Provides a free 24-hour helpline and support for children and young people; tel. 0800 1111; www.childline.org.uk

- *Young Minds:* A national charity for improving children's mental health. Parents' advice line 0808 802 5544 : www.youngminds.org.uk
- *National Domestic Violence Helpline* is available to men, women & children experiencing domestic violence, 0808 2000 247. www.nationaldomesticviolencehelpline.org.uk
- *Mumsnet:* It is a website for parents and hosts forums where users share advice on parenting and many other topics. www.Mumsnet.com
- *NSPCC:* Advice and support to parents, including online safety; www.nspcc.org.uk/parenting, tel. 0808 800 5000.
- *Parentline Plus* (part of Family Lives): A national charity offering help and information for parents, carers and families; www.familylives.org.uk, tel. 0808 800 2222.
- *The Samaritans:* Provide confidential counselling support 24 hours a day for people experiencing despair or distress; www.samaritans.org, tel. 116 123.
- *Womens Aid:* A national charity working to support women experiencing domestic abuse; www.womensaid.org.uk, tel. 0808 2000 247.

How to Find a Therapist
- *Association for Family Therapy:* Provides information about family therapy and how to find a therapist in your area; tel. 01925 444 414; www.aft.org.uk
- *Association of Child Psychotherapists:* The UK's professional association for child and adolescent psychotherapists. Use them to find a therapist in your area; www.childpsychotherapy.org.uk
- *British Association for Counselling and Psychotherapy (BACP):* The UK's professional association for counsellors and psychotherapists. Use them to find a counsellor or psychotherapist in your area; tel. 01455 883300; www.bacp.co.uk
- *Child and Adolescent Mental Health Services (CAMHS):* Your General Practitioner can refer your child to local CAMHS if you are concerned about their mental health.
- *Royal College of Occupational Therapists:* The professional association for Occupational Therapists (OTs). Paediatric OTs trained in sensory integration can support children with special needs such as autism or sensory processing disorder. Use them to find an occupational therapist in your area; www.rcot.uk
- *United Kingdom Council for Psychotherapy (UKCP):* The professional association for psychotherapy organizations and psychotherapists. Use them to find a local psychotherapist; www.psychotherapy.org.uk, tel. 020 7014 9955.

Lone Parents
- *Gingerbread:* A charity for single-parent families. It provides expert advice and practical support. It supports parents getting back to work and has nationwide self-help support groups. Helpline 0808 802 0925, www.gingerbread.org.uk
- *One Parent Families Scotland:* Offers support for lone parents and their children. Tel 080 0018 5026, www.opfs.org.uk

Practical Advice and General Support

- *Citizens Advice Bureau:* Helps to resolve money, legal and other problems by providing free, independent and confidential advice; www.citizensadvice.org.uk
- *DirectGov:* Money, tax and benefits section – information and advice on all types of benefits provided by the UK Government when you become pregnant and have a child; www.direct.gov.uk/en/moneytaxandbenefits
- *Family Action:* Provides practical, emotional and financial support to those who are experiencing poverty, disadvantage and social isolation across England; www.family-action.org.uk
- *Family Lives:* A charity that offers parenting and family support and online parenting classes; www.familylives.org.uk, helpline 0800 800 2222.
- *Home Start:* Provides support and self-help network for parents of under-fives under stress; tel. 0800 068 6368; www.home-start.org.uk
- *MIND:* Provides information, support and services across England and Wales on mental health problems; www.mind.org.uk, tel. 0300 123 3393.
- *Working Families:* Helps working parents and carers, and their employers, find a better balance between responsibilities at home and work; www.workingfamilies.org.uk; Parents and carers helpline – 0800 012 0312.

Twins and Multiple Births

- *Twins and Multiple Birth Association (TAMBA):* Provides information and mutual support for families of twins, triplets and more; tel. 0870 770 3305, web www.tamba.org.uk

Videos and Films

- *The Secret Lives of 4, 5 and 6 Year Olds* (Channel 4 TV series): Gives fascinating insight into the life of young children.
- *Inside Out* DVD: A brilliant film about feelings.
- *Parentchannel.tv videos:* Part of Family Lives, over 200 videos can be seen on YouTube. They are divided into categories of learning, behaviour and wellbeing, and separated into relevant age groups.

Part B. For People Interested in Working with Parents, Families and Children

- *Anna Freud National Centre for Children and Families:* A child mental health research, training and treatment centre; www.annafreud.org; info@annafreud.org, tel 0207794 2313.
- *Centre for Child Mental Health:* Gives information and lectures on neuroscientific and psychological research in child mental health for parents, teachers and childcare professionals; tel. 0207 354 2913; www.childmentalhealthcentre.org

- *Empowering Parents Empowering Communities (EPEC):* Supports organizations to train up parents to facilitate 'Being A Parent' 8-week parenting groups. Provides training and supervision to set up an EPEC Hub. It has a strong research base to prove evidence-based practice; tel. 0203 228 3914, contact EPEC@slam.nhs.uk
- *Institute for Arts in Therapy and Education:* Offers a wide range of training in child psychotherapy, play and art therapy; tel. 0207 704 2534.
- *Institute of Family Therapy:* For systemic family therapy training, workshops and conferences; tel. 0207 391 9150; www.ift.org.uk
- *Lantern Family Centre:* Provides therapeutic work for families and children, and parenting courses for parents. It also provides training in running parenting courses for professionals; www.lanternfamilycentre.org.uk
- *MindEd Resource:* Provides free practical e-learning sessions to help adults identify and understand children and young people with mental health issues; www.minded.org.uk
- *Parenting UK:* The national membership organization for organizations and individuals who work with parents; www.parentinguk.org
- *Tavistock and Portman NHS Trust and Tavistock Relationships:* Both provide training in working with families, children and couples; www.tavistockandportman.nhs.uk, or www.tavistockrelationships.ac.uk

How to Set up a Parent Support Group

After reading this book or completing a parenting course, you might feel like setting up a parent support group yourself, to explore child-rearing issues or hold on to some of the changes you've already made in your parenting.

I joined a parent support group after taking part in a parenting course which was an enormous source of support to me. Having now run many of these groups, I know that when the members go on to form a group, they will find it easier to get the support they need to help each other in the ever-changing challenges that parenting brings.

In order to set it up, you may want to advertise for parents to take part or ask if anyone in your network of friends is interested. The key for a successful group is to make sure that you have fun, and that everyone finds it useful. It's also useful to have a group agreement which could include rules like: no-one talking over someone else, mobiles on silent, confidentiality, starting and ending times, and no-one being judgemental so that the group feels safe for all the participants. The group will also have to decide how often they want to meet, where they want to meet, how long they want the session to be, and the best time to have the support group.

There are different formats you could use. Here are some examples.

Parent Support Group – Format 1

- **15 minutes.** Everyone sharing how they are.
- **1 hour 30 minutes.** Divide the rest of the time up between all the participants, so that they can share any difficulties or joys, and get sympathetic, thoughtful listening from all the group.
- **15 minutes.** End with feedback about the meeting and deciding on the next meeting.

Parent Support Group – Format 2

- **30 minutes.** Everyone in groups of three, and having listening time for 10 minutes.
- **One hour.** Discussion about one or two topics chosen at the previous session. Topics could range from all the different issues covered in this book, or other specific issues such as coping with bereavement, or how to help children through divorce, anxiety, sibling rivalry and screen-time, for example.
- **15 minutes.** Break for refreshments.
- **15 minutes.** Ending with feedback about the meeting and deciding the next meeting details.

Parent Support Group – Format 3

- **15 minutes.** Listening time in groups of three.
- **1 hour 15 minutes.** Discuss different parenting books, or you could ask a professional to give a talk on a topic that the whole group is interested in.
- **15 minutes.** Break for refreshments.
- **15 minutes.** Ending with feedback about meeting and deciding the next meeting details.

Having coffee, tea, juice, biscuits, fruit or cake at the break is useful in creating a good, relaxed atmosphere. Sometimes it's good to start with something the parents feel they've done well, as we so often put ourselves down.

It's helpful to have a leader who takes responsibility for the group, but this role could be rotated so that everyone has an opportunity to take it on. If you're having the support group in each others' homes, it's best to let the person whose home it is not be the leader, as they're being host or hostess and sorting out the practicalities, such as the refreshments. The leader's responsibilities are to make sure everyone sticks to the group agreement, facilitate discussions, keep track of the time, and make sure that the discussion doesn't veer off the point. The leader also has to encourage everyone to make best use of the time, get feedback on the session, and then bring it to a satisfactory end.

Listening and reflecting back what people are saying are key to making the experience helpful, and ensuring that all the parents in the group feel heard. Try to ensure that the conversation develops, with all the parents talking with each other as a general discussion, as opposed to it becoming a 'question and answer' session, with one person asking or answering all the questions.

It helps to build cohesion if the group doesn't exceed about eight people, and if the group doesn't change membership or it will no longer feel such a safe place. If a new parent does want to join the group, it's important that everyone already in the group agrees first.

The Book in a Nutshell

A short summary of each chapter, with a list of key points.

Chapter 1: Looking after Yourself

- Have realistic expectations of yourself as a parent.
- Looking after yourself (both emotionally and physically) is not selfish but vital to ensure you are able to be the parent you want to be.
- Look at your own family script for clues about the present.
- Think about patterns you want to keep and those you want to discard.

Chapter 2: Feelings

- Accept and acknowledge feelings by stating what you think the child is feeling.
- Express your feelings using the Four-part Statement, 'I feel ... when you ... because...' – and then you can ask for help to sort it out if appropriate.
- Put commands into the positive and avoid using the word 'don't.'

Chapter 3: Child-led Play

1. Children develop and learn through playing.
2. Through play children develop their creativity, spontaneity, sense of humour, desire to communicate and imagination.
3. Play helps children to understand and manage their feelings and thoughts.

Child-led Play
Spending 10 minutes a day with your child doing child-led play can give enormous positive benefits to your relationship.

- Follow the child's lead.
- Let the child decide what they want to do with the 10 minutes.
- Do a descriptive commentary of what the child is doing (some children need a lot, others just need the odd comment).
- Do not ask questions.
- Do not make judgements (praise or put-downs).
- No interpretations of what the child is doing.
- At the end of 10 minutes, do a count-down (10 to 1 with 'blast off' at the end) to finish the session, but let the child continue without you if they want to. You can also do a one-minute signal before the end.
- Even if the child has been badly behaved during the day, it is important keep child-led play and still give them the 10 minutes of Special Time. The child-led play should not be dependent on their good behaviour.

Chapter 4: Parenting Styles

There are three main types of parenting style as well as some subsidiary ones.
We all do a little of all of them, but it is helpful to be aware of what they all are and if we are tending too much to use an unhelpful parenting style.

- **Aggressive parenting** leading to unhappy children who can become aggressive themselves, angry, rebellious, scared or shut down.
- **Permissive parenting** leading to unhappy children who may feel uncared for, scared or too powerful, and who find it difficult to fit into friendship groups.
- **Assertive parenting** leading to a happy child secure in their environment, able to meet their needs and express their feelings, and let other people also have their needs met.
- **Manipulative parenting** that leads to confused unhappy children who have been on the receiving end of emotional blackmail, but are not quite able to work out how they feel.
- **Over-indulgent/guilty parenting** leads to children who can become manipulative themselves as they can see their parents' weak spots.
- **Over-protective parenting** can lead to children who are anxious and scared, or who may become risk-takers.
- **Demanding parenting** can lead to children feeling they can never be good enough and wanting to give up trying.

Chapter 5: Descriptive Praise

- Describe what the child did, and if appropriate say how you felt about it and its effect.
- Avoid put-downs or conditional praise.
- Praising descriptively gives a child an internal locus of evaluation so they are not dependent on others to feel good.
- Even children who brush aside descriptive praise will appreciate it.
- Overheard praise can be very powerful.

Chapter 6: Labels

- Labelling can create a self-fulfilling prophecy.
- Labelling can develop into roles in children which are unhelpful, especially in a group of brothers and sisters.
- Describing behaviour is much more helpful than labelling the child, as it separates the child from the behaviour.

Chapter 7: Helping Children to Solve Problems

- Helping children solve their own problems can empower them in the future.
- Creating a spider diagram with the problem in the middle and solutions on each leg can help children become creative problem-solvers.
- Parents can offer solutions as a way of giving advice which doesn't leave the child feeling defensive.
- Helping children go through the consequences of each suggestion improves their problem-solving abilities and empathy for others.
- Children learn to understand that there can be lots of solutions to one problem.

Chapter 8: The Meaning of Children's Behaviour

- No behaviour happens in a vacuum; it always has a meaning.
- There is always a need behind the behaviour, however obscure it might be.
- The commonest needs children have are for attention, belonging, security, to be able to explore and learn, to be independent, to have boundaries and to feel useful.

Chapter 9: Discipline Strategies

- Discipline means to educate, not to punish. It is an important element of socializing children and teaching them right from wrong.
- Explicit household rules ensure that children know what's expected of them.
- Routines give children a sense of security.
- Limited choice gives children agency without causing too much conflict.
- The active ignoring of petty undesirable behaviour is a very powerful way to change behaviour, as children like attention.
- Commands need to be clear, with eye contact and follow-through.
- Consequences can be natural or logical. They ensure that children grow up understanding that they are responsible for their own behaviour.
- Star charts, stickers, point systems, marbles in a jar and surprise rewards are all powerful ways of cementing positive behaviours.
- The 'Four-part Statement' is a positive assertive technique to show your children in a non-blaming way why their behaviour is causing you a problem. Use the following template: 'I feel … when you … because … How can you help me with this problem?'
- Saying 'No' is an important skill for any parent, and can be done in a firm and loving way.
- Family meetings are useful forums for discussing family concerns before they become a source of conflict.

- Negotiation can transform relationships with teenagers. Use the following six-point template: 'I'm concerned when you ... I feel ... I think maybe you feel ... This is what I would like to happen ... What would you like to happen?' Discuss the options, agree a plan of action, monitor the plan.
- Time Out is useful for 3–8 year olds as a way of exerting control when behaviour has become totally unacceptable – for example, hurting someone or breaking things. Time Out should not be used with older children if they're not used to it, as this will breed more rebellion. It should not be used with children who have attachment issues, such as being fostered or adopted, as it can trigger old memories and make the child very distressed.
- Problem ownership is a way of deciding what skills to use when there is a problem. If the problem belongs to the child then the parents needs to use the strategies that come under parent-helping skills, such as listening, acknowledging feelings and problem solving. If the problem belongs to the parent, then the parents need to use discipline strategies or negotiation skills.

Chapter 10: Ages and Stages

Child development is a process of stages that children go through. Stages help parents to know what to expect and what to do. In each of the stages, a child has to gain mastery over particular developmental growth tasks.

- **Infant, 0–6 Months: Connecting and Being.** The parent has to nurture, love and care for the baby. Much of the loving and nurturing comes through tending to the physical needs of the baby.
- **Older Baby and Toddler, 6–18 months: Doing and Exploring.** The parent needs to support and encourage the child in their explorations and keep them safe.
- **Toddler, 18 months to 3 years: Thinking.** During this stage the toddler is understanding cause and effect. They are beginning to become their own person with strong wants and desires. The parent needs to give them loving care and set limits.
- **Pre-schooler, 3–6 years: Identity and Power.** During this phase, the child is forming their identity and learning what it is to be a boy or girl. They love fantasy-play and are learning about power. Parents need to give loving care and provide strong boundaries.
- **Primary School, 6–12 Years: Structure.** During this phase, children love structure and rules. They can be a joy to teach, as they have such curiosity about the world. They want everything to be fair. As a parent, it's important to help stimulate their thirst for knowledge and creativity, and to have strong boundaries in which the child can flourish.
- **Adolescence, 12–18 years: Identity, Sexuality and Separation.** This phase is a time of great change as the young person becomes an adult with their own identity and values. They have to cope with body changes, educational pressure, peer pressure, social media, their own sexuality, and also separate themselves from their parents.

Parents need to be sensitive to their teenagers' needs, and to listen and be able to negotiate, but also be able to set limits if they feel that their behaviour could be dangerous, or not take into account the needs of others.

Chapter 11: Communication

- Communication is more than just talking; much of our communication is non-verbal.
- Listening skills can be divided into three categories: attending, following and reflecting.
- Reflective listening means to reflect back the feeling and paraphrase the content.
- The results of reflective listening are increased self-esteem, feeling accepted, and having a greater confidence in making your own decisions.
- Problems in communication can be caused by responses which are either judgemental, assert control, or are not really listening to the child's concerns.

Chapter 12: Stress Management

- Awareness of our body's physical sensations helps us to understand our feelings.
- Stress affects how we react to events.
- Letting feelings out slowly can stop an explosion of angry feelings.
- Anger often masks other feelings such as fear, shame and hurt.
- Use the image of a thermometer to imagine your emotional level – if your 'temperature' is very high, wait until you've cooled down before responding.
- It's useful to think about what triggers your anger and whether the reasons for this are still relevant.
- Finding your own ways of reducing anger is important – for example, exercise, music, reading, talking to a friend.

Acknowledgements

In writing this book there are many people I want to thank who have helped me on this journey or quest.

All the families I have worked with throughout my career who've been so committed to improving their relationships with their children. All the parent facilitators who've worked for the Empowering Parents Empowering Communities project at the Maudsley Hospital. They work tirelessly to support parents to implement changes in their family communications and provide the nurturing care and love to enable parents to feel empowered to make these changes.

For the Empowering Parents, Empowering Communities team. Crispin Day, whose support, enthusiasm, and dedication and vision throughout the last ten years have kept the project growing. Fiona Squires, Catherine Kearney, Charlotte Wilson, Laoti Adewole, Jo Nicoll, Lucy Draper, Aimee Grippman, Valerie Reed and Louise Campbell, who work so hard and with such professionalism.

To my colleagues at the Lantern Family Centre, Deirdre Dowling and Amanda Foster, who challenge my thinking and give me the pleasure and experience of sharing their professional expertise from their own discipline when thinking about families, and hence broadening my understanding. For my supervisor Linda Ryan, who always ensures I think systemically about the families I work with and provides me with a space for reflection. To Stephen Scott and Moira Doolan's dedication to the importance of parenting education in the country, whose attention to detail in analysing video tapes ensured I was aware of the importance of the smallest interaction in working with parents. For my supervision group of Surrey family therapists, Cynthia Maynard, Angela Sheppard, Mel Child, Catherine Rodger, Audrey Sandbank, Penny Mendelssohn and Gill Brown, who give such wise supervision. To the other family therapists, Judith Lask, Grace Heaphy and Joanna Pierce, Toby Humphreys and Wendy Kean, who trained me and helped me learn my trade. To my colleagues Elizabeth Baxter and Nikki Kennesion, who started facilitating parenting courses with me many years ago.

To my ex-colleagues at ACT, Amanda Carpenter, David Le Vay, Sue Pack, Amanda Hammond, Sanjit Saraw, Charnj Gill, Raphael Lopez de Soto and Daniela Kutzner, who worked with me with very traumatized children. Their expertise helped develop my thinking on the effects of trauma and loss, and the importance of prevention. Tamar Swade, the Parent Network facilitator who started my career on this trajectory, and whose love and care during the Parent-Link course embodied true facilitation skills. To Anna Clarke, whose knowledge and inspirational teaching of 'Children's Hours' has informed my thinking about supporting parents playing with their children. To Charlotte Wilson, now working at The Empowering Parents, Empowering Communities Project but also at the parenting centre, who has steadfastly kept doing the thankless tasks of keeping the Parenting Centre running. To Paul Morgan, who gave enormous help editing this book, and without whom this book would not have been produced. To Beth Shaw and Caroline Crosse, who as my children's fairy godmothers decided to support me so that I felt very cherished, and hence much more able to parent. In addition, their alternative views of what's important in bringing up children to full humanness gave me a different lens with which to understand my children. To my second family, Tola, Abiola, Elizabeth and Michael, whose survival skills and resilience have made me appreciate the power of culture, race, boundaries and love to ensure children grow straight and true.

I would like to thank Kate Hajducka, whose incredible artistic skills managed to encapsulate so many of the ideas in this book so beautifully. I would also like to thank the team at Hawthorn Press who believed in the importance of this book and worked so hard to ensure that it was beautifully produced and edited.

And finally to my own family: my parents, whose combined parenting skills and love gave me the secure base from which to explore the world and follow my own path. Their experience of immigration and dislocation, and then assimilation and becoming parents away from all family and friends, has instilled in me the importance of family and friends in the task of parenting. To my sisters and brothers Ida Fairbairn, Mike Fairbairn, David Freud and Cilla Freud, who gave me unconditional love, support and advice to help in my parenting, and my niece Anna Cooper who read the manuscript and give me helpful feedback. To my very loved children Robert (who has also been a very patient editor), Jessica and Nicholas, who inspired me on this path and who set me on this amazing journey of parenting love, and now with my children's partners Matt and Eve.

To my grandsons Harry and Raphael, who are again teaching me the fascination of the birth of relationships. Finally, my husband Lawrence, whose love, support, understanding and acceptance over the last 35 years have enabled me to follow my dreams.

Index

life trajectory, 129–30
listening skills
       'creative listening' (Pinney), 134
       teaching, 108
       see also 'fake listening'
lone parents: resources for, 141
looking after yourself, xi, 2–9
love: showing, 43
       see also attachment theory

M

manipulative parenting, 36
marbles in a jar, 79
meaning of child behaviour, xi, 56–62, 87
mentalization, 133
MIND, 142
MindEd Resource, 143
Minuchin, Salvador, 133
Mumsnet, 141

N

National Autistic Society, 140
National Domestic Violence Helpline, 141
needs, 57
negative reinforcement, 131
negotiation, 84–5
neuroscience, 13, 136–7
'no' (saying), 81
       to toddlers, 97, 98
non-blaming language, 82
non-directive play, 134–5
NSPCC, 141
nurturing parenting, 129

O

One Parent Families Scotland, 141
Oneplusone – Thinking Relationships, 140
operant conditioning, 131
over-indulgent parenting, 36

over-protective parenting, 37

P

Parent Connection, 140
parent support group
       different formats, 145
setting up a, 144–6
Parentchannel.tv videos, 142
Parent–Infant Psychotherapy, 139
parenting (styles), xi, 32–8
       aggressive, 33–4
       assertive, 36
       demanding, 37
       good-enough, 95, 130
       lone, 141
       manipulative, 36
       nurturing, 129
       over-indulgent, 36
       over-protective, 37
       permissive, 35–6
Parenting UK, 143
Parentline Plus, 141
Parents as Partners, 140
patterns in families, 4–5
permissive parenting, 35–6
person-centred psychotherapy (Rogers), 134, 136
physical health, 124
physical punishment, 90
Pink, D.H., 131
Pinney, Rachel, 134
play
       co-operative, 100
       imaginative, 100
       non-directive, 134–5
       see also child-led play
pocket money: family chores and, 80
positive behaviour
       reinforcing, 74
positive messages, 80–1

temper-tantrums, 13–15 *passim*, 24, 34, 73, 101
    fake, 67
'Terrible twos', 98
theories and/of parenting, 128–37
    attachment theory, 129–30
    communications approach, 135
    family scripts, 136
    holding relationship (the), 130
    individual psychology and discipline, 134
    mentalization, 133
    neuroscience, 136–7
    non-directive play, 134–5
    person-centred psychotherapy, 136
    proximal development, 132
    psychodynamic theory, 132–3
    psycho-social development stages, 131
    relationship education, 135–6
    social learning theory, 131
    structural family therapy, 133–4
Time In, 87
Time Out, 85–9
    exceptions for use of, 87
    how to use, 87
touch, 80
treasure baskets, 28–9
Twins and Multiple Birth Association (TAMBA), 142

U
unconscious (the), 132
unhelpful responses, 116–17
    avoiding concerns, 116–17
    judgemental, 116
United Kingdom Council for Psychotherapy (UKCP), 141

V
Vygotsky, Lev, 132

W
'When you..., then...' statement, 74
Winnicott, D.W., 130
Winston's Wish, 139
Womens Aid, 141
Working Families, 142
working with parents/families/children, 142–3

Y
Young Minds, 141

Z
zone of proximal development, 132

Other Titles by Hawthorn Press

Making The Children's Year
Marije Rowling

Drawing on the creative ethos of Steiner Waldorf education, this is a full-colour second edition of *The Children's Year*, which has been a much-loved favourite for over thirty years. From beginners to experienced crafters, this book is a gift for parents and adults seeking to make toys that will inspire children and provide an alternative to throwaway culture.

'For young children there is a sense of magic as they encounter these images, drawings and activities. Older ones will find creative projects suited to their skills and enjoyment. For adults also it offers a wide choice of craft, from tissue paper lanterns, a bee house and the old gnome, a May flower crown and lavender bags. The book aims to encourage everyone's creative expressions.'

Judy Large, from the Foreword.

240pp; 250 x 200mm; pb; 978-1-907359-69-9

Making Simple Needle Felts
Steffi Stern

Steffi Stern brings her inimitable energy and enthusiasm to her second book, intended as a back-to-basics guide to making needle-felted objects. All the projects in the book are achievable for a beginner. Some aimed at little fingers (no needles involved) and beginners, and some are aimed at those with more experience. The book is organised by season; it brims with all kinds of treasures, such as pumpkins, gnomes, strawberries, baubles, birds, bees, snails, flowers, the Nativity, mice, and mermaids. Steffi's advice is to have a go!

160pp; 250 x 200mm; pb; 978-1-907359-97-2

The Natural Storyteller
Georgiana Keable

In these pages you will find over fifty nature stories, chosen to bring both teller and listener closer to their environment. These culturally diverse stories that have stood the test of time will engage young readers, and encourage them to become natural storytellers. The stories are accompanied by tips on telling, story maps, and practical activities.

'The book is life affirming. All of its stories are about taking delight in creation. It is a journey into storytelling as well as story.' Hugh Lupton, award-winning Storyteller

272pp; 228 × 186mm; pb; 978-1-907359-80-4

An A-Z Collection of Behaviour Tales
Susan Perrow, illustrated by Allmut ffrench

Telling the right story at the right time can help children face challenges and change behaviour. All 42 stories begin with an undesirable or out-of-balance situation and, through the use of metaphor and an imaginative story journey, lead to a more desirable resolution. The stories, some humorous, some serious, are especially relevant for children aged three to nine years. They are for telling and adapting: turn them into home-made picture books or puppet shows, or even create new tales from them.

144pp; 234 × 156mm; pb; 978-1-907359-86-6

Raising Happy Healthy Children
Sally Goddard Blythe

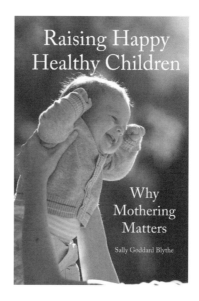

Raising Happy Healthy Children is a fully-updated second edition of *What Children and Babies Really Need.* It presents convincing research to show how a baby's relationship with its mother has a lasting, deep impact. Sally Goddard Blythe says: 'We need a society that gives children their parents, and most of all values motherhood in the early years.'

'Provides parents with the information they need to raise healthy, balanced, resilient children… Above all it demonstrates that what babies and children really need is the time, love and attention of the loving adults in their lives.' Marie Peacock, former Chair of MAHM (*Mothers At Home Matter*), from the Foreword.

260pp; 234 × 156mm; pb; 978-1-907359-83-5

Movement: Your Child's First Language
Sally Goddard Blythe

This book with 2 CDs is a collection of songs, action nursery rhymes and stories that assist child development through movement. Sally Goddard Blythe explains why movement matters for brain development, attention, co-ordination and balance. Michael Lazarev's songs help develop co-ordination and language skills.

'An inspiration … Here, you will find the simple virtues of 'music and movement' and child-raising wisdom allied with the latest neuroscientific insights to show just why the 'old-fashioned', pre-technological ways often had it right all along.' Dr Richard House

192pp; 234 × 156mm; pb; 978-1-907359-99-6

Ordering Books

If you have difficulties ordering Hawthorn Press books from a bookshop, you can order direct from our website **www.hawthornpress.com**, or from our UK distributor **BookSource**: 50 Cambuslang Road, Glasgow, G32 8NB. Tel: (0845) 370 0063, E-mail: orders@booksource.net. A full list of our non-UK distributors can be found on our website.